AN INTRODUCTION
TO
FLY
TYING

AN INTRODUCTION TO

TO

FLY

TYING

PETER COCKWILL

CHARTWELL
BOOKS, INC.

A QUINTET BOOK

Published by Chartwell Books
A Division of Book Sales, Inc.
110 Enterprise Avenue,
Secaucus, New Jersey 07094

ISBN 1-55521-558-0

This book was designed and produced by
Quintet Publishing Limited
6 Blundell Street
London N7 9BH

Creative Director: Peter Bridgewater
Art Director: Ian Hunt
Designer: James Lawrence
Project Editor: Shaun Barrington

Typeset in Great Britain by
Central Southern Typesetters, Eastbourne
Manufactured in Hong Kong by
Regent Publishing Services Limited
Printed in Hong Kong by
Leefung Asco Printers Limited

CONTENTS

FOREWORD

Fly fishing as a sport comprises of a number of linked disciplines or skills, all of which should be mastered in order to be both knowledgeable and proficient at the sport.

First we have the skill of casting, the ability to place the fly at the end of the leader exactly where we want it to be, where the fish are. The second is termed water-craft, the ability to read water to know where the fish are lying and how to approach our quarry whether we are fishing fast tumbling rivers or limpid stillwater pools. Also under the term 'water-craft' we have the skills required to manipulate a boat on some of our larger reservoirs, lakes and lochs. The next skill may, at first sight, be a little beyond most beginners, but a little knowledge will go a long way; the understanding of aquatic entomology – the ability to recognize what the trout is feeding on and being able to match a particular insect to a fly in the fly box. Last but not least we have the craft of fly dressing – the ability to create for oneself flies to tempt the trout.

No matter how good a shop-bought fly is, nothing quite compares with the feeling one gets when a trout is caught on a fly of one's own creation. An angler who does not tie his own flies can in no way be described as a complete fly fisherman.

We will never know where fly fishing started and we certainly will never know who the first person was that placed feathers and wool on to a crude fishing hook to tempt the spotted fish that rose to the fluttering insect. All we do know is that man was recorded fishing with a fly in 240 AD by the Roman writer Aelian. The fly was made with red wool and feathers from a cockerel and used on the river Astracus in Macedonia. In those days it was not a sport, but part of man's labour to provide food for his family. There are references to what could be fly fishing in earlier works but they are just passing hints, intriguing but not conclusive, so we will never know who tied the first fly.

Today fly dressing has become a very popular aspect of fly fishing with fly tying guilds and clubs throughout the fishing world. From Iceland to New Zealand and from Eastern Europe to the United States of America there are those that while away the long winter nights at the fly tying vice creating patterns to deceive the next season's fish. As they tie the basic or intricate fly, they are transported in their minds to their favourite waters as fly dressing fuels hopes and creates dreams of catching bigger fish.

Today's angler is extremely lucky for there are many courses at adult education centres or fishing clubs devoted to teaching the craft of fly tying or fly dressing. When I started out there was no such luxury. I had to teach myself from the few books that were available at that time. My first flies defied imagination but over the years they have got slightly better, and I do not mind showing them to people as they actually look like flies now.

A lot of water has flowed beneath the proverbial bridge, a mass of feathers have fluttered to the floor and more hooks than I care to count have been lost in the pile of the carpet since I first tied flies and fished with Peter Cockwill. Suffice to say that the author is one of the best fly fishermen in England today, with a vast knowledge of our sport. Why not join him through the pages of this book, at the various stages of fly tying, and become the complete fly fisherman.

There is no rule to say that a badly tied fly won't catch a fish, but through this book we can strive for perfection in our flies, and as with any skill 'Practice makes Perfect'.

Taff Price

Rainbow perfection, the author with an 18lb 14oz trophy.

INTRODUCTION

My aim in writing this introductory book on the art of fly tying is to put together the elements of the way in which I have taught fly tying to a great many people over the past 20 years and to provide the basis for many more to join the ranks of those who make flies. Men, women, youngsters and the retired and yes, even those with disabilities can all tie flies and find magic in creating a thing of beauty from scraps of feather, fur, thread and tinsel wrapped round a hook.

I have heard many reasons given to explain the desire to tie flies. They include the pure practicalities of wanting to make variations on commercially available patterns so as to achieve a better catch rate; the wish to save money by making one's own; as a way of combining an interesting hobby for the dark evenings with the sport of fly fishing; even to the ambition to tie a perfect fly just as an art form involving intricate hand manipulations.

Every person who makes flies can pitch their skills at any level of proficiency they wish but we all have to start with the basics and this book will set the reader off on the right course: after that it is up to you to decide how far to take it.

A B O V E : A 40lb King Salmon from Alaska which the Author is
about to release after an epic battle.

Fly tying may appear an immensely complex and highly skilled subject when first witnessed at, say, a State Fair or Country Show and I have often heard someone say: 'I would never be able to do such a thing, my hands are too clumsy' or that their eyes were not good enough. I will repeat that anyone who wants to and is taught properly can make flies and I know of men whose work involves the hardest manual labour and whose hands are stiff and badly cracked and yet who make the most exquisite flies and I have taught people with poor eyesigh and those who can barely peel a potato, to make flies which catch fish; the ultimate test of an artificial fly.

One thing for sure, you will always remember the first fish you catch on a fly of your own tying. Large or small, it matters not for the important thing is that the fish saw your fly as an edible item and took it. My first attempts at fly tying were without the aid of a book or any form of instruction and the resultant 'fly' was a bit of a mess but it caught me a trout from a little creek and now, 30 years later, I can still see that flash of gold as the 10 in brownie darted up from the gravel and seized my fly and made my day.

Since that day I have caught many thousands of fish on my own flies, including bluegills in an Oregon desert lake, steelheads in a Washington stream, king salmon in Alaska, brown trout from Ireland and a memorable fish indeed, the once British record rainbow trout at 20 lb 7 oz from Avington Lakes, Hants, but since overtaken by a 21 lb 4 oz fish from Loch Argyll, Scotland.

Fly tying has let me sit at a fly-tying bench alongside such greats as John Veniard and Taff Price and to fish with the legendary Lee Wulff in Africa and Jim Teeny in Oregon, as well as providing many exhilarating experiences beside river and lake which have led to lasting friendships and all with the common bond of the fly tyer.

WHAT IS A FLY?

To a fisherman the art of fly tying embraces not only the representation of actual flies but also a much wider spectrum in that imitations of all manner of aquatic life can be created, including shrimps, small fish, snails and frogs. In fact, anything that a fish might eat can be suggested by the tying of an artificial fly. There are patterns that do not actually represent any living creature but nevertheless they catch fish and because they are created at the fly tying vice they are called artificial flies.

An understanding of the main groupings of artificial flies will help to make sense of the many patterns in this book and the reasons for their construction. I divide flies into four principal groups, with the first being the nymphs.

NYMPHS Under this group come all the aquatic stages of the many flies which hatch from water and creatures which spend their entire lives underwater, such as the shrimps, hoglouse (cress sows) and water beetles. Flies tied to represent this group are mostly imitative.

DRY FLIES This group includes all the adult insects which emerge from the nymphal stages as well as terrestrial flies which find their way on to water and other land or tree-based insects which fall on to the surface . Again, flies tied to represent this group are mostly imitative although some can be said to be suggestive in that their tying does not imitate the fly but merely suggests it by the appearance of the artificial when seen by a fish below the surface.

STANDARD WETS These are the flies which in reality imitate very little and as their name implies are fished under the surface. They are mostly very old patterns which follow a basically similar format using a wide range of materials, and certainly represent something to the fish but what that is is not clear. But wet flies do catch fish and because they are a challenge to tie well they are essential work for a fly tyer.

LURES These often represent nothing that swims or lives near water because of their size and colour but they also include patterns tied to represent fish, mice, frogs and other creatures which fish eat from time to time. Many lures are often nothing more than larger versions of standard wets. Fish do take lures but whether from territorial or sexual aggression or because they look and act 'edible' we will never know. Suffice to say that fish do take lures. Why a feeding fish that will steadfastly refuse the most carefully tied and fished imitation of the creatures it is feeding on will hurl itself at a large, gaudy lure is a mystery. Virtually all artificial flies fall within these four groups and the techniques shown in this book will enable flies from all of them to be tied.

THE ESSENTIALS

There are some tools which are necessary for fly tying and it is well to become familiar with them from the beginning. At the end of the book I have listed a few additional tools but to begin with there are some that are needed to form the basis of your kit.

THE VICE

The hook has to be held firmly in order to make the operations of fly tying as simple as possible and the easiest way of doing this is is by the use of a purpose-made vice. It is true that some fly-tyers hold the hook in their fingers but I would never presume to teach anyone in that manner as it unnecessarily complicates matters.

Fly tying vices range from the cheap and nasty to wonderful precision tools, but what we require is a functional tool that holds the hook firmly and is not too expensive. For about $15 (£10) there are some super vices imported from Southern Asia which are more than adequate, and are marketed by a variety of tackle outlets. They are essentially of two types which have collet-type jaws operated by a screw or a metal lever on a cam.

A collet is a tapered and divided piece of metal which when drawn backwards through a tube causes the ends to be compressed together so that objects can be grip-

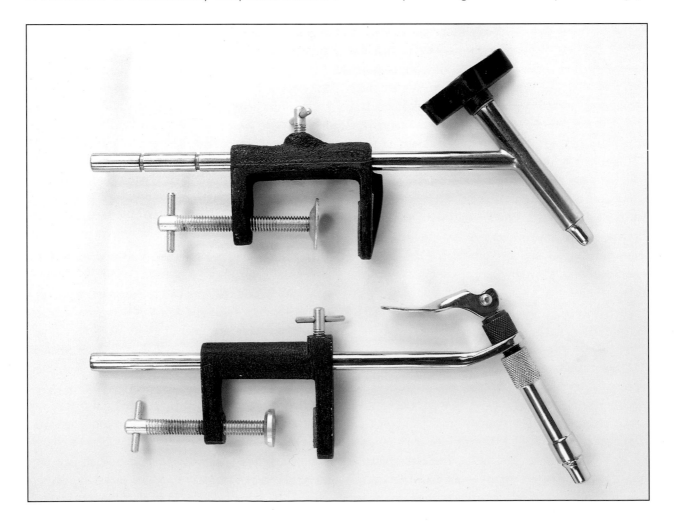

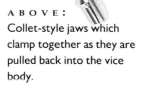

ABOVE:
Collet-style jaws which
clamp together as they are
pulled back into the vice
body.

RIGHT:
Ideal working position.

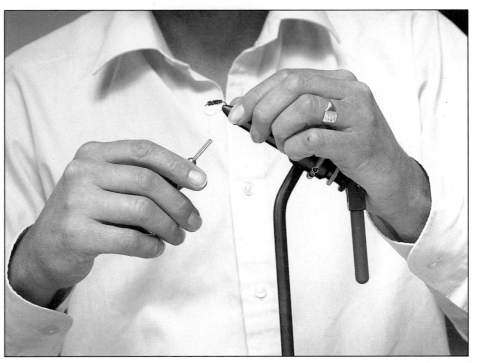

ABOVE: The all essential
scissors: here, a cheaper pair
for tinsels.

OPPOSITE: Basic vices
showing screw and lever
action.

ped. A fly-tying vice is made so that the collet ends
come together as level jaws to grip the hook securely.
Personally I think that the most straightforward system
of tightening the collet jaws is with a screw operation as
this is more positive than the lever and easier to set.
Later, you may find a lever vice to be faster and more
efficient.

The shaft of the vice goes into a clamp which can be
fixed to a table-top and it is as well to choose a suitable
work area where either good natural light falls on to the
vice or a suitable artificial light source can be positioned.
It is best to have the light coming from above and behind
on to the work area. I assume throughout this book that
the instructions are for right-handed persons but where
applicable I have included special instructions for the
left-handed.

Positioning the vice for ease of operation is largely a
matter of adjustment to your own personal posture but
generally it is best to have the vice just below eye-level
when at a seated position and about 10 in in front of
your body.

SCISSORS

After the vice — some would say before it — the next
most important piece of equipment is a really good pair
of scissors. Fly tying involves cutting fine materials with a

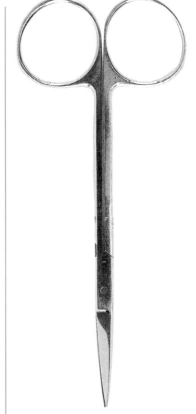

ABOVE: A fine pointed
pair of scissors for fur and
feather.

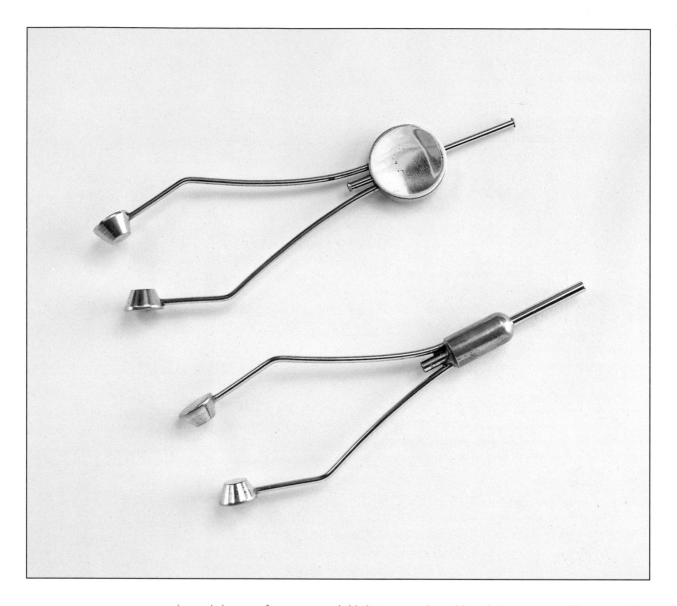

A B O V E : Two types of
bobbin holder.

good degree of accuracy and this just cannot be achieved
with scissors which are either blunt or which have tips
that do not meet properly. Invest in as good a pair as
you can afford and look after them by using them to cut
fine materials only, NEVER wire or tinsel. It is far better
to have another, cheap pair for cutting metal or coarse
material. Get into the habit right away of having two
pairs and using each for its correct purpose.

The choice of whether to have the scissors with a
curve to the tips is yours but do make sure that the tool
is not too long, 4 to 6in is about right, and that it is
comfortable to use in that the finger holes are big enough
and the cutting operation is not stiff. Check before you
buy scissors by asking to cut a single feather fibre with
the very tip of the blades. You should be able to do so
with the absolute minimum of effort.

BOBBIN HOLDER

Consider that the whole essence of fly tying involves using a fine thread to tie materials to the hook and you can understand that anything which helps to control accurate placement of the thread will be of enormous benefit. What a bobbin holder does is to grip the spool so that it will only release more thread when just enough of a pull is made to allow the spool to revolve. When allowed to hang from the hook the weight of the holder and the grip of its arms should prevent the spool from turning so that effectively the bobbin holder acts as a tension control for the thread. Also, being fed through a fine tube, the thread can be very accurately placed and if you get into the habit of holding the bobbin in the palm of your hand the tube becomes an extension of your fingers.

There are several different designs of bobbin holder so choose one that you like and which feels comfortable. Problems can occur when a sharp bit inside the tube-lip cuts the thread but the latest type have a ceramic liner which never wears and does not develop a cutting edge. I have used the simple metal ones for years and got through many spools of thread with no problem.

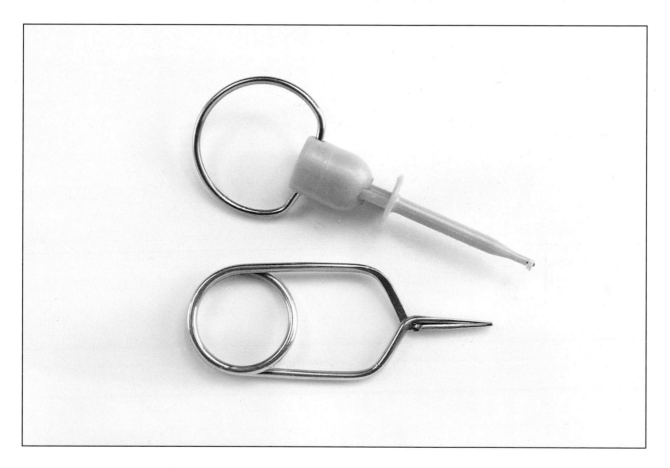

ABOVE: Traditional and Eezi hackle pliers.

HACKLE PLIERS

This is a simple little device which operates like a miniature pair of fixed-jaw pliers to grip small and delicate materials. Mostly used to grip hackles, hackle pliers are a very useful tool and there are several different designs. The conventional type has stood the test of time although I like the Eezi model where a plunger action allows a small piece of wire to grip the hackle. Relatively inexpensive, $1.50 (£1) or so, but an essential tool.

DUBBING NEEDLE

Quite simply a needle set in a handle and apart from its main use of picking out dubbed material bodies it has a host of other uses in fly tying. A dubbing needle will cost less than a pair of hackle pliers, or you can make your own.

BELOW: A dubbing needle.

WHIP-FINISH TOOL

At first sight this looks like one of those fiendishly cunning devices for making a complete idiot out of a beginner. But a well-made fly should be completed with a whip finish to give it strength and although this is possible to produce by hand the whip finish is easy when done with this remarkable tool.

These are all you need in the way of tools to make fly tying as straightforward as possible and when we move on to techniques you will see where each has its place and function. I prefer to keep my tools in a leather wallet where they are safe and always to hand, especially as I do not have the luxury of a permanent fly-tying bench.

BELOW: A whip finish tool.

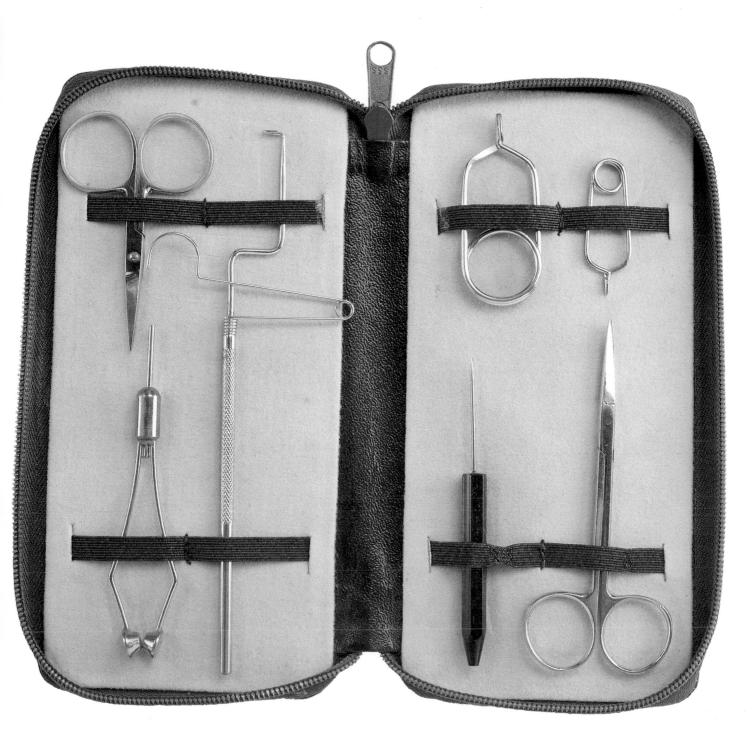

ABOVE: A zipped leather
wallet to contain the basic set
of tools.

MATERIALS

Traditionally, fly tying involves the use of a wide variety of fur and feather with the addition of tinsel in the form of wire or oval or flat section, but today all manner of man-made material is incorporated into fly dressings and almost anything can be used. An understanding of the basic feather and fur requirements will greatly assist you in coming to terms with the various stages in making flies from the four groups I discussed on page 9.

It is possible to buy kits of material which contain lots of different feathers to tie a wide variety of flies, but I prefer to start someone off with a simple selection which enables all the main techniques to be covered and a stock of flies to be acquired without any great initial expense. Many once widely used feathers are now extremely difficult to obtain and indeed it is often illegal to trade in the plumage of certain protected bird species which at one time provided plumage in common usage for a great many patterns.

As anglers and fly-tyers we should be seen to be fully aware of the pressures on the world's wildlife and our interests should not in any way endanger a species.

RIGHT : A magnificent Jungle Cock neck.

LEFT: A selection of
natural coloured necks
(capes).

Where therefore it was once acceptable to use, say, feathers from a jungle fowl we must now use a substitute or feathers from birds reared specifically for the purpose. You might be surprised to learn that many birds are reared to supply the fly-tying market, so great is the continual demand for plumage.

Feathers that fly-tyers use more than any other are hackles from ordinary poultry. These are the neck feathers from the cock and hen birds and there are many colour varieties. Good quality hackles are becoming increasingly scarce and there are not enough naturally occurring necks from free-range birds to supply the world demand. This has led to poultry being reared just for their neck plumage and genetically engineered and bred to provide the perfect hackle. No wonder that such feathers may well be very expensive, but at least they are available.

The well-known Metz hackle from the US is a prime example of perfect feather production for the fly-tying market. Also, too, with the ban on culling young seals there is now very little seal fur available for fly-tying but perfectly acceptable substitutes are available from a variety of commonly occurring fur-bearing animals so that there is no need to use the original material specified for so many patterns. It is no disaster, for the fish cannot tell the difference!

RIGHT: A very high
quality 'genetically' produced
Grizzle neck.

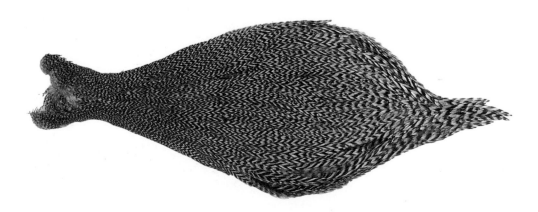

A good basis to begin fly tying includes the following selection of materials in addition to the range of tools already listed:

1.   A spool of ready-waxed tying thread
2.   A natural brown hen neck
3.   A dyed black hen neck
4.   A natural red game cock neck
5.   A dyed black cock neck
6.   A cock pheasant (rooster) centre tail feather
7.   A bunch of peacock herl
8.   A set of grey mallard flight quills
9.   Three packets of seal's fur substitute
10. Three lengths of wool, red, black, fluorescent green
11. Spools of medium width gold and silver tinsel

ABOVE: The necessary basic selection of materials to start fly tying.

12. Spools of fine gold and silver wire

13. A dyed or natural black squirrel tail

This is not a very long or exhaustive list of materials but with it you can tie known patterns which encompass all the techniques described in this book and then add other materials to make up the patterns which you might want to tie. Get the basics right and you can then make any fly.

My suggested starter list of materials as shown opposite may seem strange, so I will discuss each item in turn so that you will begin to understand the terminology of fly tying and some of the reasons for the items listed.

1. Traditionally, fly tying was done with silk thread and, later, cottons and synthetics which were rubbed with a soft wax as the fly was being made. The wax helps the thread to stick to the hook and materials without unravelling as each stage is done. Nowadays we use synthetic threads of incredible strength for their diameter and which are prepared ready-waxed.

2. This is the neck or 'cape' taken from a hen bird and it will have a variety of hackle sizes on it. A plain brown is as useful as any to start with and is cheap. The accompanying photograph shows a complete hen-neck with a large and small hackle from it alongside. Look at the individual feathers (as shown in the photograph opposite) and you will see that a hen feather is wide and rounded and appears soft, while the cock feather is sharp and narrow and looks spiky. Hen feathers are mostly used for flies which will fish under the surface (wet flies). Cock feathers are tied on flies to be fished on the surface (dry flies), their stiffer, spikier fibres enabling the fly to sit on the surface-tension. A similar fly made with hen hackle fibres cannot support itself and will soon sink.

Become familiar with the look and feel of hackles and you will soon be able to differentiate them. A really good quality cock neck would have all the feathers, from the very smallest upwards, of identical coloration and marking. Each feather would be long and slim and very short in the fibre and there would be a high proportion of small hackles. Necks like this are reasonably common in the natural reds but exceedingly rare in colours such as Furnace (red game with black centre and black tips) or Grizzle (black and white barred). A good natural black is also difficult to obtain but one can make excellent dyed black necks by using a natural red as the base colour, for there are plenty available.

3. That is why this one is listed as a dyed black hen as it will be much easier to obtain than a natural one and considerably cheaper. A black hen neck allows many wet flies to be made.

4. Plenty of natural red game necks are of good quality. This feather makes excellent dry flies and is also used as tail whisks. Remember this one, you will use it more than any other.

5. A natural black cock neck is a rare thing but once again the dyed natural red saves the day. An extremely useful feather, a black cock hackle is especially good for dry flies and also for some lure tyings and other functions.

6. Roosters are not so common in the US but in Britain, where the driven bird is the basis of the big estate shoots, the common pheasant is reared in huge numbers. The famous Teeny Nymph is often tied from English feathers as I send many thousands across the Atlantic each year to my friend Jim Teeny. The two centre tail feathers are used to make the Pheasant Tail Nymph which has world-wide appeal as a basic nymph imitator,

BELOW: A cock neck showing small and large hackle positions.

but the fibres are also used for tails of larger dry flies or when knotted as legs for terrestrials such as the Crane Fly.

7. Where would fly tyers be without the tail plumage of the gorgeous peacock? The bushy, shiny green feathers make excellent chunky bodies when wrapped round a hook and stripped of their flue (the little fibres clinging to the central stem) make a marvellous segmented effect for a dry fly body.

8. Grey mallard flight quills are taken from the common mallard, either male or female, but most common wild ducks provide a grey flight feather. It is the ideal one with which to learn winging for it is a strong feather and holds its individual fibres together very well. The important thing about winging is that you must have a feather from each wing of the bird in order for them to make a pair, much as a left and a right hand make a pair, two lefts do not match up. It is the same with bird feathers. Being flight feathers they have very efficient hook and-eye systems to hold each fibre together. They therefore hold well when being tied to a hook. An ordinary plumage feather will not have such strong links for each fibre and when you use, say, bronze mallard and summer duck the feather has very weak fibre links and is therefore much harder to use as a winging medium.

9. A seal's fur substitute will allow dubbing to be learnt. There is no better way to create a shaggy body effect on a fly to give an illusion of bulk, and at the same time allow light to pass through, than when using individual hairs trapped by turns of thread. Olive, brown and black will allow several different patterns to be made and form the basis of a collection of dubbing materials.

10. Wool can be used to form tails, tags of bodies on flies and all sorts of colours can be used. The three suggested will enable you to make a lot of very effective patterns.

11. Medium-width tinsel allows for bodies to be made which reflect lots of light and many standard wet flies use tinsel bodies. Learn to use tinsel properly and very smart flies can be tied.

12. Wire makes an excellent ribbing material on a fly body both to give strength and weight to the pattern and to supply the all-important segmented effect which is attractive to a trout. Look at most insects and you will see that they are segmented. Copy this and your fly begins to look lifelike.

13. Wings made of hair are very common on artificial

BELOW: The very clear difference between a cock and hen hackle.

flies and there is a separate technique for applying it. Squirrel tails are easy to use and very common and a natural or dyed black will enable you to make many patterns.

Once you use these materials you will be fascinated, and begin the process of becoming a dedicated fly fisher. It will not be long before other materials get added, some of which will be used on a regular basis and others which will be there just in case or because they look good. The original storage box overflows into a series of boxes, and then into a proper chest of drawers and then a roomful! Scavenging of odd bits of material from friends' houses begins and you start to acquire a reputation as the strange, ghoul-like person who stops to retrieve bits from animals and birds killed on the highway. It is all good fun and part of the mystique.

PROPORTIONS

The most common theme in my method of teaching fly tying is continually to emphasise the need to get the dressing of a fly put together in the correct proportions, by which is meant the relative length of, say, the hackle and tail to the size of hook being used and the insect or creature being imitated. It is true that greatly exaggerating the size of one portion of a fly will sometimes enhance its attractiveness to a fish but usually it is better to keep all the elements of the dressing in proportion.

Referring again to the four principal groups of flies it is fairly easy to prepare a representative diagram of each and indicate the correct proportions.

Starting off with group 1, the nymphs, this is a diagram of a typical nymph dressing. It is shown alongside a drawing of a natural Ephemerid nymph and I hope that you see the similarity. Of course, the copy does not resemble the real insect but the proportions are right:

(a) The natural insect has a segmented abdomen, almost always seven segments, and the artificial should suggest this with its ribbing of the abdomen.

(b) The natural has its abdomen about twice as long as the thorax — look at the artificial!

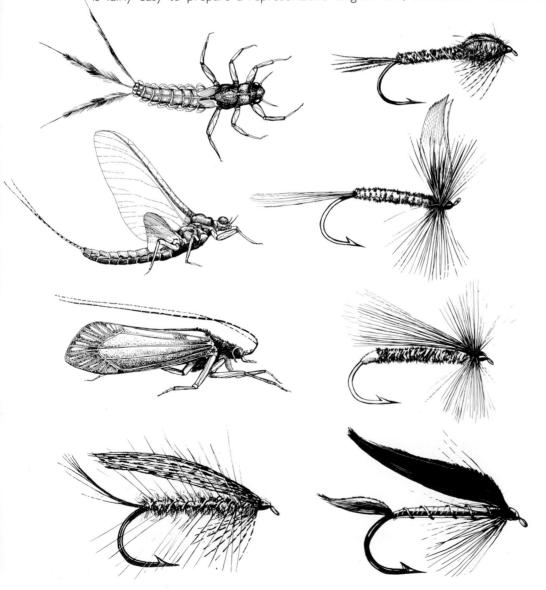

An Ephemerid nymph and a standard imitation.

An adult Ephemerid and a split wing dry fly.

A typical Caddis fly and the fly tyer's imitation.

Standard Wet Fly Dressings. Invicta and Butcher.

(c) The natural has a tail roughly the length of the abdomen and its legs are also the same length. The fibres we use to suggest the tail and legs therefore need to be in proportion.

(d) The natural has a distinct hump to its thorax, this is where the embryo wings are housed. Our imitation has the same pronounced hump.

Moving on to group 2, I have shown a typical upwing adult Ephemerid against the fly tyer's suggestion and a roof-winged caddis fly against its artificial. Look at the segmentation, length of wings, angle of wings, thickness of body and length of legs, and the absence or presence of tail. All are in proportion to the natural creature.

Group 3 is slightly more difficult to explain because here we are not imitating any specific form of life but suggesting by virtue of colour and form that the artificial we have created appears edible. There are, however, certain ground-rules with regard to proportions on standard wets that if adhered to will make the fly not only very attractive to look at from our human, aesthetic point of view but also appealing to the fish.

The diagram shows two typical standard wet fly dressings. Notice how certain elements of the artificial are kept in proportion to a natural insect even though this type of fly rarely actually imitates one. The ribbing of the abdomen again shows seven segments. The tail, wing and hackle lengths are relative to a natural, so once again we are working on correct proportions. Finally, to group 4, the lures.

Most flies in this category represent nothing but, as has been said earlier, they are often little more than enlarged standard wets and again therefore the same standards of proportion apply. Look at the drawing of a typical hair-wing lure and you can see immediately the same proportioning as the standard wet.

A streamer pattern or Matuka follows much the same idea but enlarges one element, in this case the wing length.

A Muddler originally intended to imitate a minnow (in Europe Phoxinus; in the US a number of small baitfish), so a drawing of the Muddler and the original minnow shows just how far away from the original theme some Muddler patterns now are. And they all of them catch fish!

Lures with mobile tails, called leeches in the US, and Nobblers in the UK, rely on a very long tail of soft material, either man-made or natural, to give the lure a

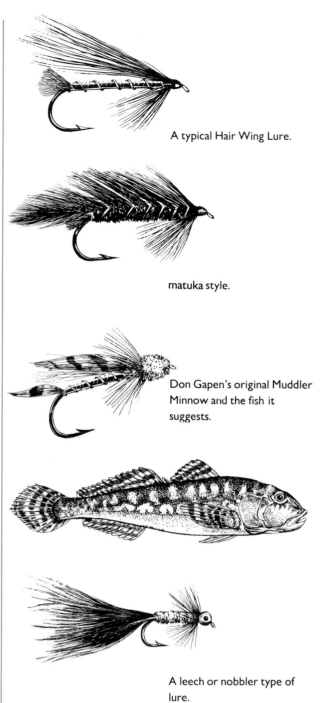

A typical Hair Wing Lure.

matuka style.

Don Gapen's original Muddler Minnow and the fish it suggests.

A leech or nobbler type of lure.

wriggling, pulsating movement when retrieved. A brilliant imitation of a black leech, but what does a magenta pattern suggest? Goodness knows, but at times the fish will impale themselves on it. Even a wiggle-tail fly has to have the correct proportions or it will not work properly when retrieved. A 2 in tail pulses; a 4-in one wiggles. When we move on to actual techniques I shall continually refer to the need to get the correct proportions, so read back over this section. It is very important.

HOOKS

Without a hook we have little chance of catching a fish and there are now hundreds of different hook patterns all based on a pointed, bent and barbed length of wire. Modern fly tying is done with an eyed hook either straight, up or down-eyed depending on personal preference for the type of fly being tied. The length of the shank can vary tremendously as can the gape of the hook and the set of the point. Hooks come either plain or forged, the latter having the bend compressed to give it more strength. The modern trend in fly fishing is to use barbless hooks so that an unwanted fish can be released with the minimum injury and so provide future sport. However, the vast majority of fly hooks are barbed and a range of commonly used patterns is shown.

Hooks are tempered in that the metal is heat-treated to harden it, but tempering is an absolute science for the hook must not be so brittle that it breaks when under tension, i.e. when in the mouth of a fish, and nor must it be so soft that it straightens out under a pull.

If as a fly tyer you are going to spend a considerable amount of time constructing a fly on a hook then the first thing you should do is to test its temper. If you do not, then your own temper is likely to be very severely tested if after much effort and time the hook breaks or straightens on the first fish it hooks. However, testing a hook takes but a moment and you do it as soon as the hook is placed in the vice.

At this point you will learn how to place a hook correctly into a fly-tying vice. The object is to cover the point of the hook with the jaws of the vice so that the tying thread does not catch on the sharp point and cut it. The hook must also be held so that the shank is level to make the tying operation easier and you do this by getting a good hold with the vice jaws on the lower part of the bend. Do not screw up the vice jaws so tight that the face of the jaws can be damaged, use just enough grip to ensure that the hook is firmly held.

The temper-testing operation is not too technical, all you do is to depress the hook end with your thumb and let it go. If the hook bends or breaks discard it and try another. Ideally, it should return instantly to its original shape with a 'ping'.

The old adage that you get the best by paying the most applies very much to hooks but even then you will get the occasional bad one in a batch.

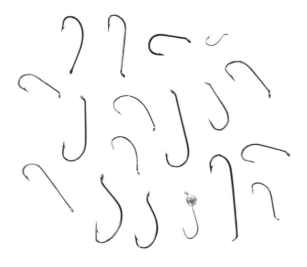

ABOVE: A wide selection of the many hook patterns available.

ABOVE: The basic selection of hooks, size 12 sproat down eye, size 10 limerick down eye, size 12 sproat up eye, size 10 perfect long shank.

Fly tyers have an enormous range of patterns from which to choose and there is a pattern for every conceivable fly within the different patterns made by Eagle Claw of the US, Mustad of Norway and Partridge of England.

To start fly tying I suggest that you obtain a packet of 25 each of the following hooks:

Size 12 Sproat bend standard-length shank, down eye.
Size 10 Limerick bend standard-shank length, down eye.
Size 12 Sproat bend standard-shank length, up eye.
Size 10 Perfect bend long-shank, down eye.

With this selection you can tie nymphs, dry flies, standard wets and lures and then, later on, you can make other flies on patterns of your own selection or based on the recommendation of the tyer who originated the fly you want to make.

Look after your hooks by keeping them dry: corrosion is a terrible thing for fishing hooks and has been the cause of many a lost fish. A small compartmented plastic box makes an ideal storage container, with the advantage that the hook types are readily seen. Make sure that the lid fits securely, for one day you will drop your hook box and it is not much fun picking them out of the carpet and sorting out several hundred different hooks into sizes and patterns. It teaches you all about hooks, but what a way to learn!

With a little knowledge of hooks and one of a suitable temper in the vice now is the time to move to the first proper stage of becoming a fly tyer.

ABOVE: The correct position of a hook in the vice.

LEFT: How to test a hook for 'temper'.

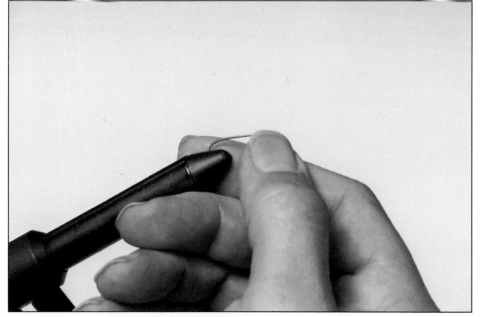

TECHNIQUES

Here comes the difficult stuff! How do you get all those little bits of feather, thread and tinsel on to a half-inch-long hook and make it look like a fly worth putting on the end of your line? Remember what Taff Price said in his Foreword about his first flies being absolutely dreadful and how I said the same thing in the Introduction about my own early efforts?

You now have the benefit of both mine and Taff's experience and the fact that we have tied many thousands of flies and taught each other – and a great many other people – how to share this super hobby of fly tying.

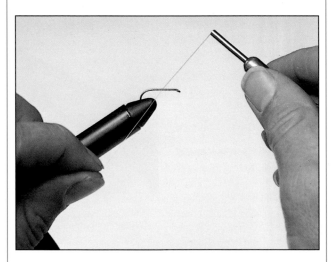

LEFT: Tying thread crossed over the shank.

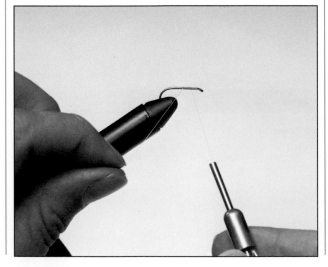

LEFT: Four turns of thread towards the eye.

Take a Size 10 standard-shank hook and put it in the vice. We are going to learn how to start and finish the fly before any material is applied to the hook.

Most books on fly tying tell you to lay the thread on to the hook-shank in touching turns from the eye to the bend. However, other than for very fine tying I have never believed in doing this and all I want to teach you is how to make flies to fish with. If you want to go on to perfection of technique later on then that is the subject of another book. Now we are going to tie flies.

With the bobbin held in the right hand and about 4-in of thread protruding from the bobbin, take hold of the end of the thread with the left hand and place your hand at the lower axis of the vice as shown in the photographs opposite and below.

Lay the thread on to the hook shank roughly midway and take four even turns round the shank, going away from the body and working towards the hook eye.

RIGHT: Four turns back to the bend and the thread is attached.

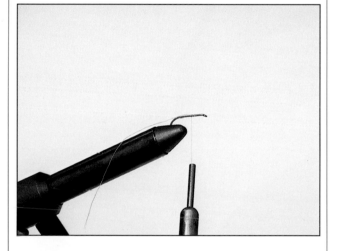

RIGHT: Hand whip finish.

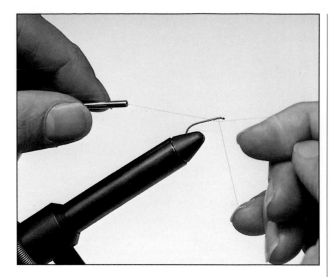

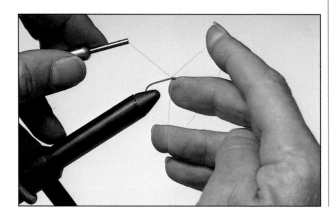

Stop and then take four more turns going back down towards the bend so that you cover the previous four turns. Now you can let go of the thread in the left hand and allow the bobbin to hang down below the hook and the thread will stay in place. That's it, the first stage is over: you have the thread on the hook.

Next, take the thread down towards the bend and back up towards the eye, not necessarily to form a base for the dressing but more to get the hang of holding the bobbin and using the end of the tube as though it is your fingers to get very accurate placement of the thread. Take off the thread and do the whole thing again and end up with the bobbin hanging off the hook just down from the eye.

Cut off the waste end and run the tying thread up to the hook eye. Having started the fly we are now going to finish it. It might seem odd but the hardest thing you will learn is how to finish a fly properly. It is no good having got to the stage of completing the dressing of a fly and then finding out that you do not know how to finish it off! Learn the whip finish technique and you will have no further problems with fly tying. There are two ways of doing a whip finish, one is with your hands and the other is with a tool. At first, both seem impossible but if you follow these instructions and refer constantly to the photographs you will have no problems.

T O P : With a clockwise rotation of your hand and using the forefinger as a lead you trap the thread from the bobbin against the hook shank with the loop in your fingers.

A B O V E : Still using the forefinger to maintain loop tension, the other two fingers now press on to the bark thread of the loop so as to turn the thread around the shank.

R I G H T : The loop is now brought down below the hook with all three fingers, now moving to press on what is the front thread of the loop. The forefinger again takes the lead to bring the loop of thread up over the hook once more.

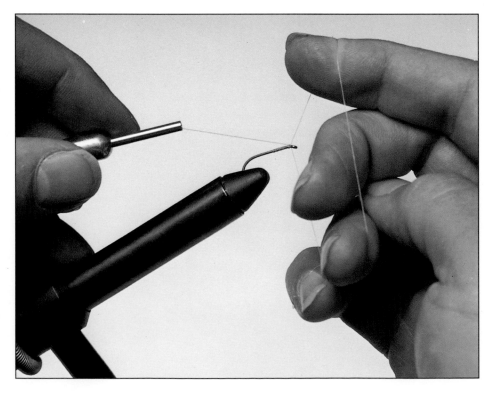

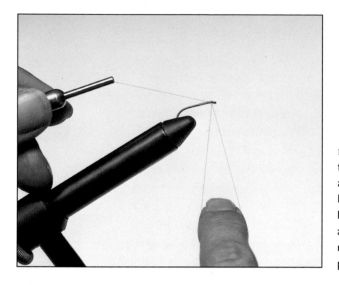

LEFT : When four or five turns have been wrapped around the shank, the loop is brought down below the hook and just the forefinger and thumb can pinch the remains of the loop until it is pulled tight.

RIGHT : Pull the bobbin gently and the loop will be pulled towards the hook shank until the forefinger and thumb can pinch the remains of the loop until it is pulled through.

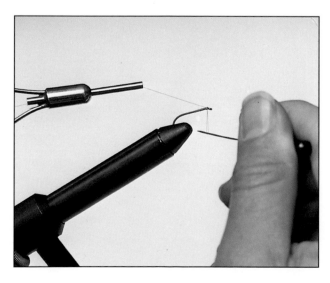

BELOW : Alternatively, you can use the dubbing needle to control the loop being pulled in tight.

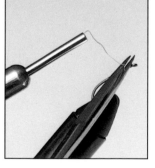

LEFT : Scissors cut off the thread and the completed whip finish is the most secure way to finish off a fly.

THE WHIP FINISH TOOL

I do not know who the American was who invented this twisted bit of metal but he must have been a genius. But you must learn how to use the tool properly. I recall one fly-tying class where I decided to teach the whip finish instead of the hand method I had previously taught. But I had never actually used a whip finish tool, rashly assuming that it would be easy. I felt somewhat foolish having to admit defeat and go away to learn the technique before the next class!

The tool has two loops, one large and one small. Make sure that the bobbin has released about 10 in of thread and hold it in the left hand at the base of the vice stem. With the tool in the right hand you now place it behind the thread and engage the large and small hooks in the thread as shown. Now move the left hand up so that it is level with the tool and at all times maintain tension on the thread, not too much but just enough to keep it taut.

Bring your right hand up so that the tool is horizontal and begin to turn it in a clockwise direction towards the hook. The thread coming from the hook and held by the small loop will now touch the thread being held by the bobbin in the left hand and a simple figure 4 appears.

BELOW: Engage large and small loops of tool from behind thread.

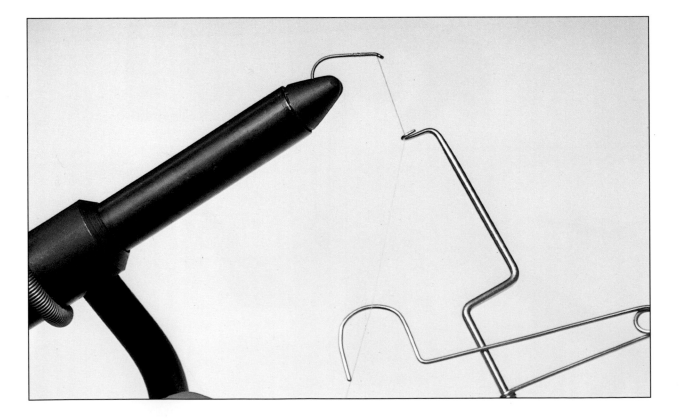

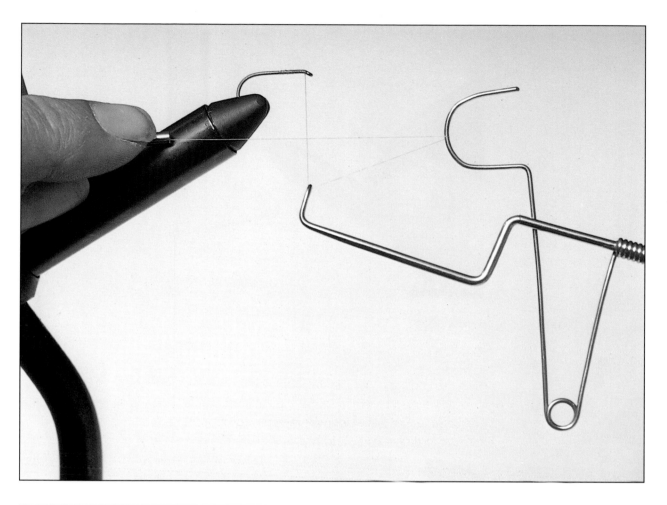

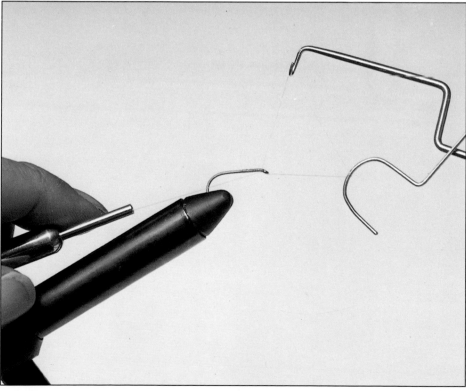

ABOVE: Rotate tool clockwise while raising it to horizontal so that the figure 4 is formed with the thread.

LEFT: Continue to rotate clockwise until loop of thread controlled by small loop of tool traps thread from bobbin against hook shank.

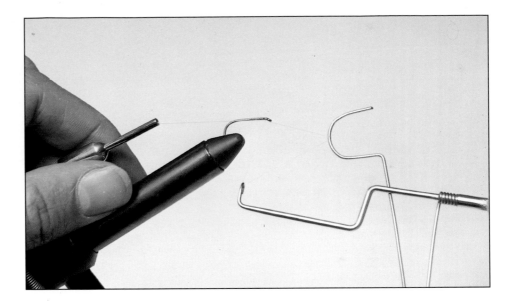

RIGHT: Turn the tool around the hook while also rotating it clockwise so that samll loop always has bend facing the hook.

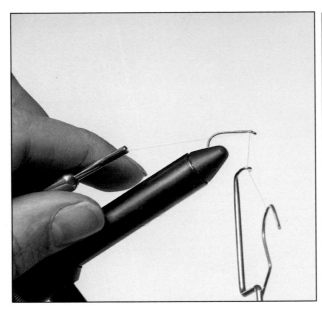

ABOVE: After four or five turns bring tool down under hook and at right angles to it.

You must now concentrate on the thread being controlled by the small loop of the tool. Continue to rotate the tool clockwise so that it becomes trapped against the hook shank. The left hand can rise during this process until it is level with the hook. You should now be at the situation shown in photograph (x). The small loop is now controlling the process and in order to get it to wrap the thread round the hook shank and so round itself it is now necessary to turn to tool round the hook and at the same time slowly rotate it in the same clockwise direction so that at all times the bend of the little loop faces directly toward the hook. Fail to do that and the thread will disengage from the loop.

Do about five turns round the hook shank and then bring the tool down under the hook so that the thread is now at right-angles to the shank. It is nearly all over!

Slip the small loop off the thread so that it is now only held by the large loop. If you now gently pull to the left with the left hand the loop of thread being held by the large loop of the tool will be drawn in towards the hook. When the tool butts up against the hook you disengage the large loop and pull tight with the left hand. That's it, you have now completed a whip finish. Properly tied with waxed synthetic thread a whip finish is strong enough to last the life of the fly without further protection, but it is usual to cover the thread with varnish to seal it and give a smooth finish.

The whip finish is by far the best way to complete a fly and much more secure than a series of half-hitches. Take the trouble to learn it and you will save time and money in the long term as well as having a well-tied fly.

L E F T : Disengage small
loop of tool.

R I G H T : Pull gently
on bobbin so that large loop
of tool is pulled up to the
hook shank then disengage it.

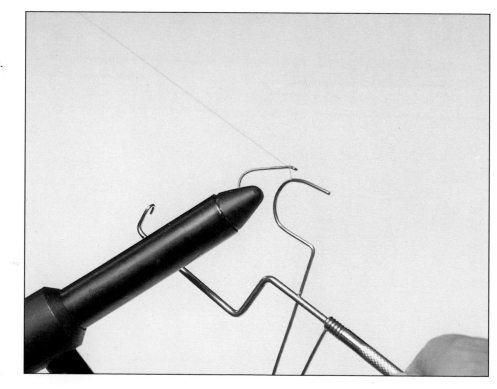

Wild brown trout from Lough Melvin in Ireland.

MAKING YOUR FIRST FLY

Get to the stage of a hook held securely in the vice and the tying thread secured to the hook shank. We will start off with a pattern made from feather fibre for the body. It is better to start by doing this as you immediately get used to handling feather rather than strong wool. Take two fibres of peacock herl and cut off the curly end where the fibre was attached to the main quill and then line up the two cut ends in your left hand so that about half an in of material projects from between your finger and thumb. Offer this up at an angle to the hook and just touching it.

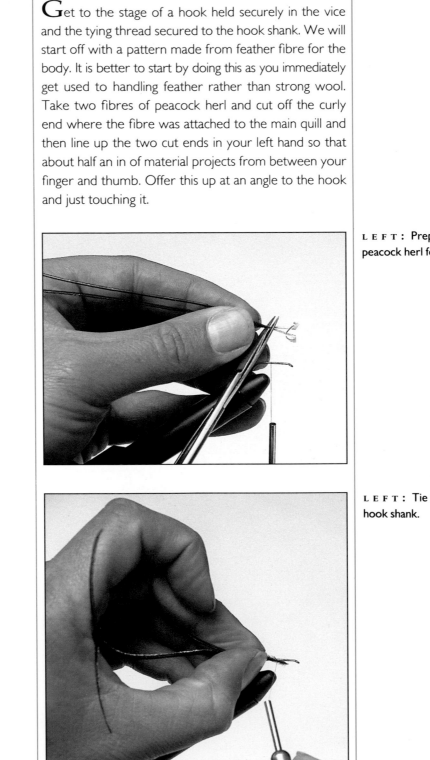

LEFT : Prepare the peacock herl for tying in.

LEFT : Tie the herls to the hook shank.

Holding the bobbin in your right hand raise it up and round the hook and all the time maintain tension on the thread. As the thread comes up round the hook shank it will cross the ends of the two sections of peacock herl and trap them against the hook. Carry on round the hook shank with the thread and twice more wrap it round the peacock fibres. You will always be turning the thread over the hook away from your body in a clockwise motion.

Having secured the body material to the hook the usual step would be to take the tying thread up towards the eye of the hook and then wrap the body material round the shank. Peacock fibre is, however, rather a fragile material and the first fish caught on the fly will invariably cut one of the fibres with its teeth. Consequently, the fibre will then unravel and very shortly you have no fly.

RIGHT : Herls and tying thread held together.

RIGHT : Winding on the body and the twist develops.

We are now going to strengthen the body material of this fly by taking the two fibres of herl into the right hand along with the tying thread and commence winding them all round the hook shank, working first down towards the bend and then back up towards the eye so as to build up a nice, chunky body. After about the fourth turn round the hook you will notice that the herls are twisting and that the thread is twisted with them. As you wrap this twist round the hook, each herl is being trapped by the other and by the thread, so if the herl should become cut it cannot unravel because it is trapped by so many turns. This is the way to get a good, strong fly which will last for more than one fish.

At this juncture I am going to stress the first of the points about proportioning.

It is vital that as you attach each piece of material to the hook you take note of how it will appear at the final stage. For example, even with such a seemingly simple operation as attaching two strands of peacock herl and making a body, it is important that the body starts and finishes at defined points on the shank of the hook. There is only going to be a herl body on this fly, so the twist should be taken down to the bend of the hook to fill the level section of shank. It should finish at the end with sufficient room left to make a hackle and a whip finish.

Probably, the most common mistake you will make is to leave insufficient room at the head of the fly; this not only makes it very difficult to finish the fly but it appears very crude and introduces a weak point where it can become undone.

A correctly constructed and proportioned fly not only catches fish more efficiently but it 'looks' right. You will soon be like every other fly tyer: when a fellow angler looks in your box and asks where you buy your flies you will look smug and say 'Actually, I make my own!'. So now we have a well-tied body of peacock herl on the hook and if we add a hackle the fly will be born and usable.

For this, our first-ever fly, it is going to be a wet fly that will be fished underwater and therefore the hackle to use is one from a hen neck. It will easily absorb water and sink, whereas a cock hackle would be all stiff and spiky and prevent the fly from penetrating the surface film.

Use a dyed black hen hackle and the fly will be a recognised pattern called a Black and Peacock Spider, a

ABOVE: A correctly proportioned body with room left for the pattern being tied.

R I G H T : Selecting a hackle of the right fibre length for the pattern being tied.

A B O V E : How to remove a hackle from a cape.

R I G H T : Removing the fluff from the base of the hackle prior to tying in.

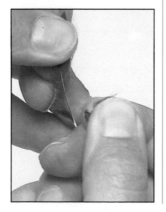

very effective artificial. Look at your black hen neck and you will see that at the base, which is the top of the bird's head, the hackles are short and have short fibres, while those at the other end of the neck are much longer and have correspondingly longer fibres.

A hackle must be selected that will have the correct fibre length for the size of fly being tied. Proportioning again!

Refer to the drawings of a standard wet fly and you will see that the hackle fibre length is slightly longer than the total shank length. Therefore we need a hackle with fibres of these proportions for the hook in the vice. Instead of randomly taking a hackle off the neck and finding that it is not right it is better to offer the whole neck up to the hook and bend out individual hackles until you have one that is right and then pluck it off the neck. Do this by gripping the hackle at its base and pulling it towards the base of the neck, away from its natural growth line, and it will pop out of the skin.

The hackle must now be prepared before it can be tied to the hook and this involves stripping off the downy fluff from either side of the base of the stem so that only the actual fibres proper are left. Do this by gripping the fluff each side of the stem and pulling down and away from the stem.

L E F T : Attaching the
hackle to the hook shank.

T O P : The natural curve of
the feather shows the correct
way to tie it in.

A B O V E : The wrong way
to tie in a hackle.

Now hold the prepared hackle up between finger
and thumb and you will see that it has a distinct curvature
and a face side which is on the outside of the curve. If
the hackle is tied to the hook and wound so that the
curve points towards the eye, the fibres will all slope
that way and the fly will look unnatural and oppose the
water as it is retrieved, rather than envelop it by curving
over the hook.

Correctly positioning the hackle before attaching it to
the hook overcomes this problem and it is a matter of
offering the prepared hackle up to the hook so that its
face is towards you and the natural curve of the feather
is over the top of the hook. Look at the photograph
above and it is very clear.

Now trap the hackle stem against the hook shank in
the same way as you did the peacock herl stems. The
tying thread should be on the hook-eye side of the
hackle at this point.

This is where we introduce another tool, the hackle
pliers. They act like a spare pair of hands and grip the
end of the hackle very firmly. Hold them in line with the
stem of the hackle and grip the last quarter-inch.

Now wind the hackle round the hook shank in the
same direction as the tying thread, i.e. over the body
going away from you and in a clockwise direction. Do
not twist the hackle but keep its face side pointing at the
hook and eye and make each turn at the same place on
the shank. Do not let it wander about to cover a long
area, keep it compact.

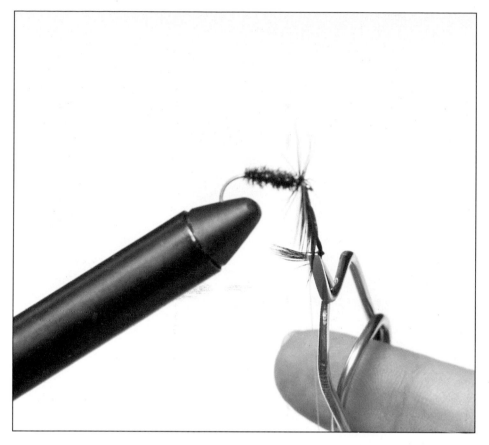

L E F T :
Winding the hackle with the
aid of hackle pliers.

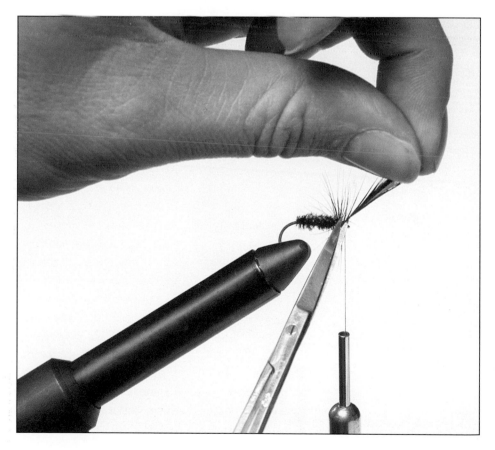

R I G H T : Cutting off the
waste tip of the hackle.

R I G H T : The inevitable odd bits of feather fibre projecting at all angles.

B E L O W : Using thumb and first two fingers to stroke back the odd bits of fibre.

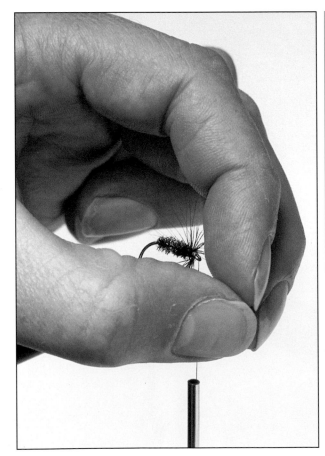

Do about four turns of the hackle and now finish with the hackle pointing down from the shank. Cross it over in front of the tying thread and lift the thread up and over the hook to trap the end of the hackle against the hook. Do a couple of turns over the hackle and you can now carefully cut it off. Use your best scissors and snip the stem close to the hook, but be careful you do not cut the thread as well.

The fly is now virtually complete but before you do the whip finish, which you learnt in a previous section, you will need to tidy up the head of the fly because there are almost always a few odd bits of hackle fibre sticking out at the wrong angle, making the whip finish difficult to carry out.

I tidy up by touching the tips of my thumb and first two fingers of my left hand together, leaving a small gap between them. Then slip this finger/thumb pinch over the eye of the fly and slide it backwards down the body of the fly. Bits of fibre will be stroked backwards, allowing you to take a couple of turns of the thread over this last section to trap them in a backward-sloping profile and leave the way clear for the whip finish.

That is it, your first fly! Now go out and catch a fish on it.

A final professional effect can be created be applying a coating of dope to the whipping. There are several proprietary products for this final stage, some take the form of a varnish which sets like rock and is called head cement. The kind of dope used by model-aircraft makers is perfectly all right for the job and if you apply it with the point of the dubbing needle it will go on very evenly and accurately. Try putting on a layer of black dope and when it is dry add a layer of clear. This gives a shiny head to the fly just like those commercial patterns.

You have now learned to make a simple fly and can put on a herl body and a wet fly hackle, so now it is time to move on to another stage.

A B O V E : The completed head of a neat fly.

L E F T : Varnishing the whip finish.

RIGHT: Attempting to trap the wool against the hook shank.

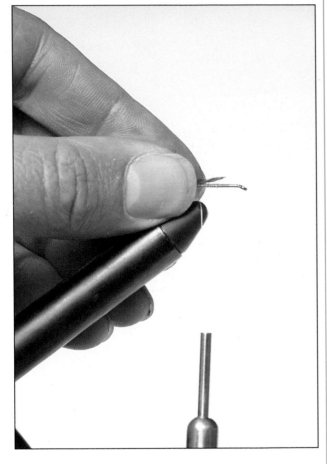

ABOVE: Tying thread at the correct position prior to tying in the tail by pinch and loop.

THE PINCH AND LOOP

This is a technique used to get a piece of material to sit exactly square on the hook shank and it must be mastered or you will never be able to do winging. We are going to start by using the pinch and loop technique to put a wool tail on to a fly.

Try cutting off a section of red wool, an inch will do, and then tying it to the hook shank so that it sits exactly on top of the shank and faces backwards as a tail.

So far we have applied a few bits of herl to the hook and then wound over them to make a body. Try tying the wool tag in the same way by offering it up to the hook and bringing the thread up over it to trap it to the hook. What happens is that the thread pushes the wool round the hook and no matter how quick you do it the wool ends up at an offset angle to the hook and not symmetrical as it should be to make a nice effect and to get the fly to move through the water properly.

The pinch and loop technique will solve this problem and enable you to tie material on to the body of a fly exactly where you want it. First, you need to decide where the tail is to be tied in. It seems obvious — it should be at the end of the fly, but what it means is that the tying thread should be at the point where you want to tie the tail and not still part way up the hook shank. So, having attached the thread to the hook you must now run it down towards the bend of the hook and stop just where the hook starts to bend.

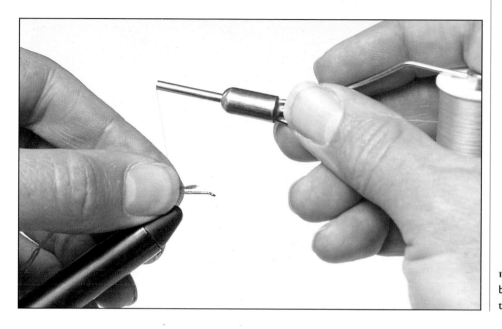

L E F T : Bring the thread up between the hook shank and the thumb.

R I G H T : Loop the thread over the top of the hook and the wool tail and down between finger and hook shank.

Now, hold the piece of wool between the finger and thumb of your left hand and offer it up to the hook so that the wool is lying level with the hook and on top of the shank as in the photograph on page 44, left. Lift the tying thread up so that it slides between the thumb and the wool. Bring the bobbin over the top of the hook and back down the other side so that the thread now slides between the finger and the wool. Now pinch the lot together and if you slacken off the tension on the thread from the bobbin nothing will come loose as it is all being held by the pinch of finger and thumb, which now has a loop of thread going up over the section of wool. Hence the term pinch and loop.

If you now hold the bobbin below the hook shank and pull downwards while still keeping pressure on the

A B O V E : With everything firmly pinched pull down the loop to trap the tail.

L E F T : Trimming the wool tail off to length.

pinch, the loop will slide down between your finger and thumb and trap the wool against the shank of the hook. Do the loop operation again without moving your fingers other than slightly to relax the pinch and again pull tight. Now, if you remove your finger and thumb you will see that the wool is square on top of the hook and exactly positioned to be the tail of your fly.

You can now trim it to length, repeat the operation done on the first pattern and apply a body of peacock herl. Make sure that the turns of herl-twist butt up exactly to the tail where it is tied on and do not overlap it, twisting the tail off-centre. Complete the fly by putting on a hackle from the natural brown hen neck and you now have a wet Red Tag. This is a very famous old trout fly which is also excellent for catching grayling.

BELOW: Herl body butted up exactly to where the tail is tied in.

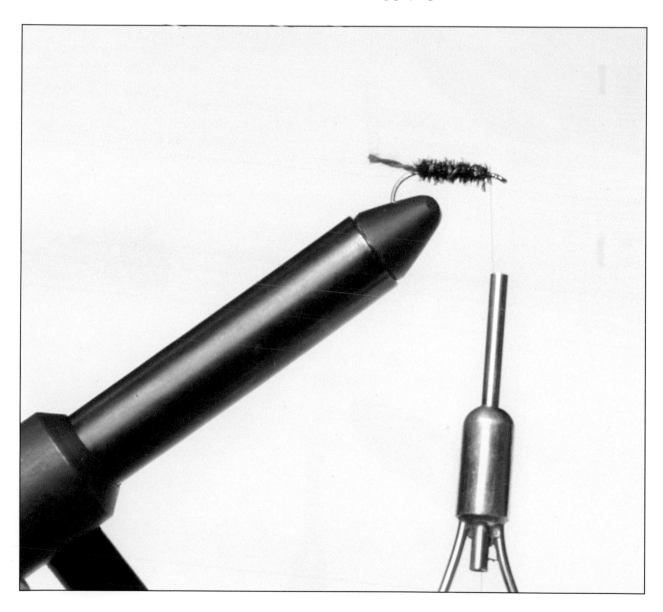

RIBBING

Remember how in the section on proportions I emphasised the importance of the segmented effect in fly tying? You can achieve this by ribbing the body of a fly dressing with a thread or tinsel and no matter whether you are making an exact imitation dry, a simple nymph or a large lure it is always best to aim for the natural look of segmentation and go for six to seven sections in the body. In due course you can gradually increase the width of space between each ribbing turn to more exactly copy nature. It is surprising how much better your fly will look when correctly ribbed.

Let us tie a fly with a rib based on the work we have already mastered.

Start off with pulling a tail of bright green or fluorescent wool and then cut off a 3 in length of silver wire, tying it in by one end so that the long end projects back like a very long tail. Do not just catch the very end of the wire but get at least half the hook shank to tie the wire to so that it is securely trapped. Now make the peacock herl body just as you did before and ensure that sufficient room is left at the head of the fly, because we now have to tie in a piece of wire as well as the hackle.

A B O V E : A length of wire ribbing tied in.

R I G H T : Ribbing up the body.

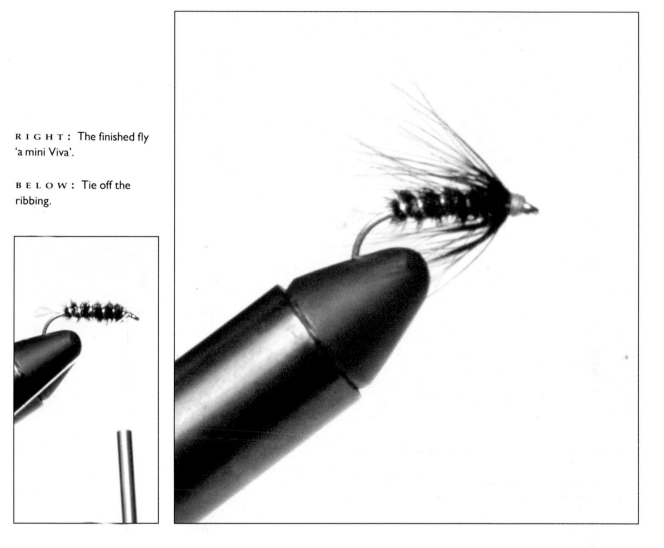

RIGHT : The finished fly 'a mini Viva'.

BELOW : Tie off the ribbing.

With the body complete you now leave the bobbin holder hanging from the eye end of the hook and grasp the wire between thumb and forefinger of your right hand (using the hackle pliers if preferred).

Instead of winding the wire up the hook shank in the same direction as in every other operation you must now wind it anti-clockwise round the hook. This is done so that it will cross the body material in the opposite direction to the way in which it had previously been tied. Not only will it (the ribbing) further strengthen the body, it will also stand out as a rib rather than be hidden by sliding between the turns of body material. This is particularly important when using thick and bushy body material which would otherwise obscure the rib and lessen its impact on the dressing of the fly involved.

Having now run the wire up towards the eye of the fly with the spacing as even as possible, you can you now take the bobbin holder in the left hand and put a couple of turns of thread over the wire to secure it in place. It will sometimes try to unravel itself as it has been wound against the normal pattern of tying, i.e. anti-clockwise instead of clockwise, so it is wise to turn the wire back over the top of the hook shank and bend it back towards the tail section and tie over it again. This produces a double lock to ensure that it does not unravel.

You can now cut off the waste end of the ribbing wire and proceed to add a hackle. If you put on a black hen hackle you will have tied a mini-lure.

A black fly with a green tail is often deadly for trout but I have no idea what it represents to that fish. Already, then, we have made a Black and Peacock Spider, a wet Red Tag and a small lure, often referred to as a Viva.

By using various combinations of the materials in the basic kit you can make a number of well-known patterns all of which you could use with confidence.

TINSEL BODY

This stage will introduce a new element into our fly dressing repertoire in that neatness of tying will now be rather more important than before. We are going to make a standard wet fly which has a body of flat tinsel and to get that to look first-class it is necessary to think carefully about the final effect.

Ideally, the fly should look like the one in the photograph. The tinsel body starts exactly where the tail of the fly is tied in and then runs in a smooth, even way to the hackle. Unless the bed over which the tinsel is to lie is itself flat then the tinsel has no chance. If you make any kind of step in the body the tinsel will have to follow that contour and spoil the overall effect. The hungry trout will not notice it, but good tying techniques at this stage will make life much easier for you later on.

With this fly we will try another material and make the tail from feather fibre.

Pick a hackle from the end of the neck which has the long-fibred feathers. Use the red game cock neck as this will have nice, straight fibres to the hackle and make a neat tail.

A B O V E : An uneven bunch of fibres plucked away from a hackle.

If we want to make a good fly, it will look so much better if the fibres of the tail all line up at their tips, and this is the way of ensuring that they do.

If you hold the hackle in your right hand, face towards you, and grasp about half an inch section of fibres on the left side of the feather with your left hand and pluck them down and away from the stem of the feather you will see that the tips are all uneven. It would be very difficult to try to line them up now, so discard that feather. Now hold the tip of the hackle in your right hand and run your left thumb and forefinger down the spine of the hackle.

LEFT: Stroking the hackle fibres will let the section plucked away have the tips of equal length.

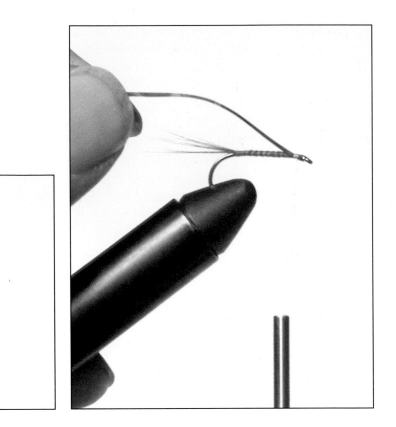

ABOVE, LEFT:
Fibres of cock hackle tied in
for a tail.

ABOVE, RIGHT:
Tie in the tinsel for the body.

RIGHT: Run the tinsel
down to the tail roots.

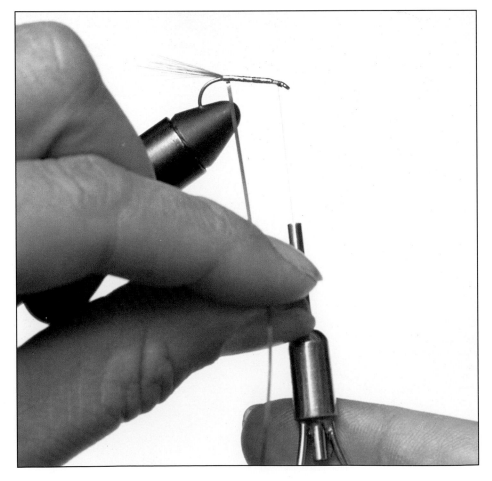

This will have the effect of making the individual fibres stand out at right-angles from the spine of the feather. You might have to stroke it a couple of times to make them all line up properly. Now take another half inch section of fibres between the thumb and forefinger of your left hand and pluck them away from the centre spine of the feather. You will find that all the tips now line up.

This little bunch of fibres can now be offered up to the hook and tied in with a pinch and loop so that about a length equal to the shank of the hook will project back from the tying-in point. Running along the back of the hook shank will be the remainder of the bunch of fibres. Cut them off at the point level with where the tinsel body will end up near the eye of the hook. Now take turns of tying thread up the hook shank towards the eye and tie down these ends of fibre.

Cut a 3-in length from the spool of flat gold tinsel and tie in one end as in the photograph opposite, right, with the long end projecting back towards the tail. Hold the tinsel again either in finger and thumb or with the aid of

the hackle pliers and wind it down in roughly touching turns towards the tail. When you get to the tail it is most important that the last turn of tinsel exactly touches against the tail fibres. Not just short of them, so that turns of thread show, and neither just over the tail so that it is forced off its position on top of the hook shank and immediately prior to where the bend begins.

Now you can run the tinsel back up towards the eye of the fly, again in roughly touching turns, and then tie it off just as you would a hackle end. You will now have a perfectly smooth, flat tinsel body running from the tail to near the eye. All that remains is to tie-in a hackle from the natural red hen neck and finish off the fly. You now have a simple wet Wickham's Fancy. This is a very old pattern and effective for many species of game fish.

If you wish to make the artificial stronger you could add a gold wire rib and run it up the body in an anti-clockwise spiral, but make sure that when you tie it in the end of the wire rib is tied down level with where the tinsel body is going to finish or you will be introducing a step in the body which will spoil its looks.

A B O V E : Back up towards the head to show the lovely flat effect.

R I G H T : A hen hackle finishes off the tinsel bodied fly.

PALMERING

This is a technique in which the hackle is wound along the body of the fly to give it more bulk and a lifelike effect. It is not difficult to master because you have already learnt how to tie in and wind a hackle.

To make a simple fly such as a Palmered Wickham's, which is a super dry pattern, we will need to start off as in the previous pattern and put on a tail of hackle fibres from the cock cape and then before winding up to the eye of the hook you must tie in a length of gold wire to form the ribbing. Tie it so that as you wind towards the eye you are covering the wire all the way and then there will be no step in the body. Tie in a length of flat gold tinsel and as before wind it down to the tail root and over the wire before winding back up to the eye and tying off.

Now select a feather from the cock red game neck which has the correct fibre length for the hook gape, i.e. just longer than the actual gape. Trim the base of the feather and then stroke the fibres down from then tip towards the base so that they stick out at right-angles from the stem. This makes it easier to wind the hackle for the palmering stage. What you should now have is a

ABOVE: Preparing a hackle for palmering.

RIGHT: Tie in the hackle, the ribbing material is ready at the tail.

length of wire projecting from the tail of the fly and a hackle at the head held by its root.

Grip the hackle tip with the hackle pliers and take a couple of turns round the head as though you are doing a normal hackle and then wind it down towards the tail of the fly in open turns. Do this carefully, keeping the hackle straight and being careful not to twist as you wind.

When you get to the last turn immediately before the tail, you leave the hackle pliers on and hanging down from the hook. Now take hold of the wire, either in your finger and thumb or with a second pair of hackle pliers, and wind it anti-clockwise up the body towards the eye just as you did for the previous ribbing exercise. Make sure that the fibres of the hackle do not get trapped by the wire as you wind, only the hackle stem should be crossed by the turns of wire.

You can use the dubbing needle at this stage and flick the fibres free from the wire as you wind. When the wire gets to the head of the fly, tie it off just as you did the ribbing and end with a whip finish. You can now carefully cut off the stem of the hackle where it is held by the pliers and you have tied your first palmered fly. Congratulations!

ABOVE: The hackle wound down towards the tail to show palmering.

LEFT: The ribbing traps the final turn of the hackle and crosses it all the way up the body.

RIGHT: Offering up the bunch of hackle fibres which will make the 'false' hackle.

FALSE HACKLE

Tying-in a false hackle is a prelude to making a winged standard wet fly but at this point we are discussing variations on a theme as you can already tie thread to a hook, do a whip finish, attach materials, wind a hackle, do a pinch and loop and make a rib.

Refer to the previous section and put on a tail of feather fibre and a body of flat gold tinsel; then turn the hook upside down in the vice so that it is the same as in the photograph.

Now prepare another long-fibred hackle from the red game cock neck and take a rather larger bunch of fibres than you used for the tail. These are going to be the hackle and will be tied in on what is the underneath of the hook shank to fill the gape of the hook just as a fully wound hackle would, except that we are only using some fibres and hence the hackle is a false one. The reason why we do this will soon become apparent.

Offer up the bunch of hackle fibres so that the ends project to just beyond the hook bend and then tie in the bunch with a pinch and loop so that it sits exactly on what will be the underneath of the hook shank. Carefully trim off the waste ends and turn the hook the right way up in the vice.

Look at the upper surface of the hook shank and you will see that it is flat and level with the tinsel body. Had we wound a full hackle and then tried to bring the fibres down underneath the hook shank, by tying over those on the upper surface, there would inevitably have been a bump at this point, which would seriously hinder the next operation, which is that of winging a wet fly.

L E F T : The 'false' hackle tied in.

W I N G I N G

This is where your careful learning of the pinch and loop technique really comes into its own and it is the only way you are going to get wings on to this fly.

First, select a pair of similar-sized wing quills from the grey mallard set. It can be seen from the photograph below, left, that the two mirror-image feathers make a pair. We take a slip of fibre from each quill and put them together to form the wing for the fly.

Selecting the width of a slip of fibre might seem difficult but a rough rule is to make the width about half the hook gape. You can use the dubbing needle to

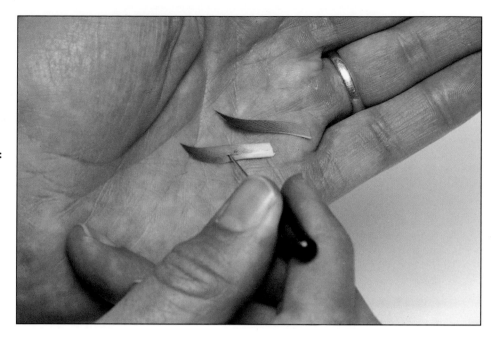

OPPOSITE, LEFT:
A pair of grey mallard wing quills.

OPPOSITE, RIGHT:
A slip of feather removed to make a wing and showing its natural curve.

separate the individual fibres so that the section of fibres you want is clear from the rest, then cut it clear from the feather shaft. Take another section of fibres from the same place on the shaft of the other feather in the pair and now you have two wing slips ready for tying in.

You will quickly realise that you can cut out a section of the fibre without having to be too accurate in gauging its width. If you now look at the two wing slips you will see that each has a curve to it and that if you line up the tips and make them into a pair you will find that when held one way round the natural curve of the slips makes the tips of the pair separate, and held together the other way the natural curve holds them together. It is this latter position we want for a wet fly pattern, while the former is used for split-wing dry flies. These are discussed in the next section.

Already you will have discovered how tricky it is to get the two wing slips to line up exactly level with each other and how it is all too easy to spoil them while attempting it. Here is another very useful piece of advice.

Pick up the wing slip with the curve which when laid in the palm of your left hand will sit with its two ends up in the air. Now put the other slip on your hand so that it is the other way round so that its ends are touching your skin. Take the dubbing needle in the right hand and carefully pierce the second wing slip in its middle. Lift up the needle and the wing slip will stay on it.

Very carefully place this over the top of the other slip and then press the needle point down until the second

ABOVE, TOP: How to pick up wing slips with a dubbing needle.

ABOVE: The two wing slips perfectly matched and ready to be tied in.

slip is also pinned through. You can now lift up the needle and the two wing slips will be exactly positioned together. Grasp them with the finger and thumb of your left hand and there is your first pair of wing slips ready for tying in.

The next stages are explained as clearly as possible and you must note every instruction carefully or the wing of your fly will never sit properly. Ideally, we want it to be on the top of the hook shank and exactly in line with it and also set low so that there is very little gap between wing and hook. The photographs show the perfect set for wet-fly wings and achieving this is entirely dependent on how you use the pinch and loop to put the wings on.

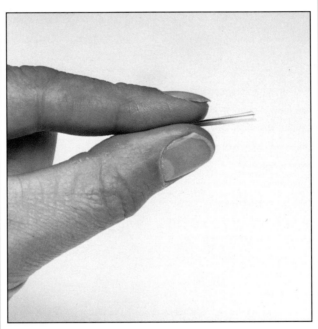

L E F T : Finger and thumb straight to show the pinch.

First, take a look at the photographs of my fingers and you will see that above I have a finger and thumb straight-jointed and that where they pinch together there is a vee-shaped gap towards their tips. If you now look at the photograph opposite, left, where I have bent the finger and thumb joint you will see that the pinch has now moved farther towards the tips. I call this 'increasing the angle of the pinch'. The next photographs show the line between the pinched finger and thumb and if you know that the wing slips will be in this pinch, and hence in this line, then wherever the line of the pinch is seen that will be the line along which the wing will sit when tied down.

If you set the pinch at an offset angle to the hook

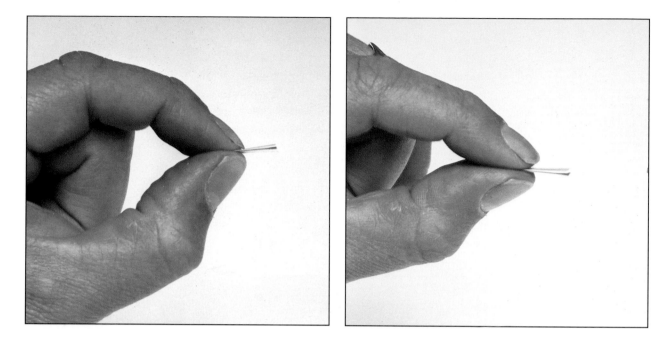

ABOVE, LEFT: Bend the joints and the length of pinch changes.

ABOVE, RIGHT: The line of pinch between the finger and thumb determines exactly where the wing will lie.

shank then the wing will also be at an offset angle. This is the most common fault in winging and one that is seldom understood. The line of the pinch must be exactly above and absolutely in line with the hook shank. Please read through this last section again and make absolutely sure that you understand it.

Now, with the prepared pair of wing slips between finger and thumb of your right hand you must offer the wings up to the hook shank and position them so that the tips project to just beyond the bend of the hook and that they lie parallel with the hook shank and exactly on top of it. Now grip the slips with your left thumb and finger.

Lift the tying thread up between thumb and wing slips, loop it over the top and then down between finger and the slips. Increase the angle of the pitch by bending the joint of the finger and thumb and at the same time ensure that the line of pinch is exactly on top of the hook and dead in line with the shank.

Pull down with the bobbin and the loop of tying thread should now slide down between your pinched finger and thumb and press the wing-tip down on to the hook. You will see the root ends of the slip kick up in the air as they are caught up by the thread.

Without relaxing your pinch, repeat the process to put another turn of thread over the slips and then remove your pinch. Hopefully you will now see your first-ever wing sitting proudly to attention.

Assuming that the wing looks pretty good you now

take it in a pinch again and put a couple of turns of thread round the base of the slips to secure them, and then while still holding the pinch get your best scissors and cut off the waste ends. If you cut off the ends without holding the wings you risk pushing them off-centre, because you cannot cut with exactly equal force on each blade of the scissors. All that now remains is to do a whip finish and the fly is complete. Congratulations, you now have a wet Wickham's Fancy!

The ability to make a winged wet fly that is correctly proportioned and with the wing absolutely on top and in line with the hook shank is one of the fundamental assessments of an accomplished fly tier.

ABOVE, TOP LEFT: The pair of wings offered up to the hook and the tying thread in the correct position.

ABOVE, TOP RIGHT: The loop pulled down between the pinch and the end fibres kicked up.

ABOVE, LEFT: Holding the wing in order to cut off the waste fibres.

ABOVE, RIGHT: The completed winged wet fly.

DRY FLY WINGS

~~~~~~~~~~~~~~~~~~~~~~~~~~~~~~~~~~~~~~~

At this point, refer to the chapter on proportioning and look at the length of wing slips on a typical dry fly and the hackle fibre length as well as the way the whole fly is constructed. There are several ways to make a dry fly and I believe that the following method will quickly get you into making perfectly acceptable patterns.

Take a dry fly hook, the up-eyed one, and put it in the vice. In fact, there is very little to choose between up- or down-eyed hooks for efficiency of use in dry-fly fishing but there is no doubt that a dry fly does look better tied on an up-eyed hook.

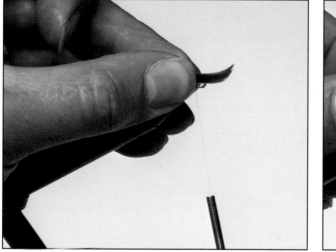

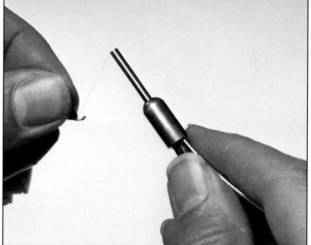

ABOVE, LEFT: Wing slips offered up in the reverse position for a dry fly.

ABOVE, RIGHT: Lift up the slips and take two turns of thread at their base.

LEFT: Separate the slips with a dubbing needle.

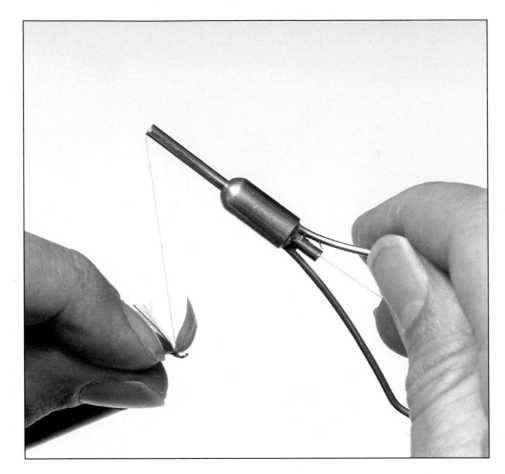

L E F T : Pull one wing slip down and take a turn of thread between the wing slips.

A B O V E : A turn of thread from the opposite direction between the wing slips.

Run-on tying thread, take it down to the bend and attach a few cock hackle fibres with a pinch and loop, a technique which should have become routine. We are going to make a quill-bodied fly which can successfully imitate many of the adult up-winged flies and at the same time acquire another tying and handling technique.

Material required for the body is the familiar section of peacock herl, but this time stripped of its flue. Get these off the stem by pulling the piece between finger and thumb with the nail of the thumb pressing on to the stem, which effectively rubs the fibres off. It will be necessary to do this a few times to ensure that you get a clean de-fuzzed stem.

Look at the piece of peacock quill and you will see that it has a light and a dark side, so that when wound along the hook shank it will give a segmented effect.

Tie in the piece of prepared peacock quill at its thinner end and just where the tail of the fly is tied off leave it projecting over the end of the fly. Now run the tying thread up to about a third of the shank length from the eye of the hook. Do not take it too close because a lot of work has yet to be done.

A B O V E : Cut off the wing
roots at an angle.

Now prepare another pair of wing slips from the
mallard quills, but this time when you put them together
to make a pair you will do so in a way that allows the
natural curve of each slip of feather to curve away from
the other. The tips of the slips will now be separated.

Take the pair of slips and reverse them so that they
now appear to be back-to-front for tying in. The tips
should be projecting over the eye of the hook rather
than down towards the bend as in wet-fly tying. Offer
the two slips up to the hook and ensure that the length
of the wing will be correctly proportioned when tied in,
i.e. about one-and-a-half times the hook gape.

Perform the same operation as for tying-in the wing
slips on a wet fly and when you have done, use the
pinch and loop securing turn of thread, release the pinch
and make another turn over the roots of the slips; this
time it will be down towards the bend of the hook and
not towards the eye.

At this point you must ignore the supposed fragility
of feather fibres. With your left hand hold the wing slips
and bend them backwards towards the bend of the
hook. Take the tying thread and make two turns round

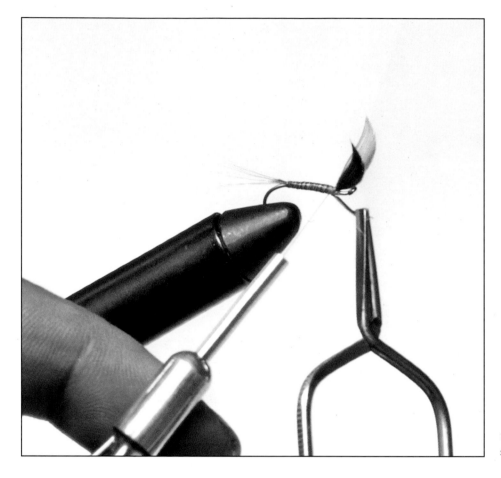

LEFT: Wind up the
stripped quill body.

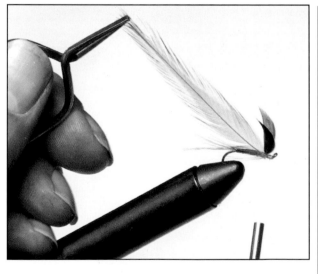

ABOVE: Tie in a cock
hackle.

the hook shank immediately next to the slips on the eye-side of them so that they will now be held upright. The two slips will probably have stuck together while you did this, so separate them, very carefully by inserting the tip of the dubbing needle between the two slips to press them apart.

Now take the nearest one in your left hand and bend it away from the other so that you can bring the tying thread up between the two slips and to the rear of them. Let go of the wing slip and take a locking turn round the hook at the rear of the slips. Now take the other wing slip, the one farthest away from you, and again bend it away from the hook.

Bring the tying thread up between the slips, this time you will be coming from the rear, and again take a locking turn round the hook and in front of the slips. It sounds rather complex, but what you now have is the two wing slips firmly tied on in an upright position and separated by a criss-cross of threads. They are now perfectly safe and cannot be affected by any other operation. It is far better when tying a dry fly pattern to get the winging bit over at an early stage.

Now it is time to cut off the wing roots, but here it pays to be crafty and cut them at an angle so that the ends actually taper back towards the end of the hook. This makes it much easier to form the body of the fly because there is no step in it. Take a few turns of tying thread over the wing-roots to make them into a neat taper. Tie off against the hook shank and return the tying thread to the actual wing base.

Take the end of the quill between finger and thumb and in touching turns run it up towards the wing base and tie it off. That makes the body of the fly. It now only remains to tie in the hackle. It should not be too difficult, you have done it several times before.

Prepare a suitable red game cock hackle, its fibre length a little more than the gape of the hook, and tie it in by its base. Grip the end with the hackle pliers and take two turns round the hook shank on the eyed side of the wings. Now run the hackle under the hook shank and take two more turns round the hook at the rear of the wings so that they end up looking as if they are surrounded by hackle fibres. You can generally finish by doing a few more turns of the hackle at the eye side of the wings before tying off and completing a whip finish.

BELOW : Wind on the cock hackle either side of the wings.

As the hackle fibres should be sticking out at right-angles from the hook all round the eye area, you might find it better to pull the hackle fibres out of the way over the body of the fly while you do the whip finish. It is amazing what you can do with the dry fly once those wings have been put firmly in their place.

As has been said earlier there are several different ways of tying dry fly wings and with different materials, but this is a classic way and by now you must wonder what all the mystique is about dry flies.

HAIR WING

Hair is a very different material from feathers, for although it is constructed from the same base, keratin, it is not compressible. Unlike feather fibre, it is difficult to get a firm grip on hair with tying thread and we therefore need to use a different technique when tying it in. Some hair is easy because it is hollow, but most hair, and the type we are using, is made of a solid shaft. Running through a simple lure tying we can use the long-shank hook as the starting base and make a larger version of the Viva we made earlier in this book.

BELOW: A squirrel tail with the hair pulled at right angles to the bone to even up the tips.

ABOVE: Pulling the short hairs from the section of hair to be used as a wing.

First, tie in a length of the fluorescent green wool to act as a tail and then a 3-in section of flat silver tinsel and a similar length of black wool. Make sure that you tie in so that the body can be bound over a level bed. Run the black wool up towards the eye and tie off when it is about three-quarters of the way up the shank, and then follow up with silver tinsel on the opposite spiral. Cut off the waste ends and then tie-in a false hackle of long black cock fibres. This now leaves the way clear to tie in the hair wing.

It is time to become familiar with the black squirrel tail. It is very much like a feather in construction in that it has a central stem, the bone with the fibres coming off at an angle. If you stroke the fibres away from the bone and in a downward direction you can again line up the tips just like we did with the hackle fibres.

RIGHT: Offer the hair wing up for length.

Do this with a section of the hair, a bunch about as thick as a Biro refill will do, and then cut it free from the bone. If we were now to tie in this section of hair it would almost certainly come loose at some time because the long hairs would not be firmly enough gripped by the tying thread. The reason for this is that with the long hairs, known as guard hairs, is the under-fur which is a much softer, shorter-fibre hair. Tie it all in together and you will find that the longer guard hairs are not gripped firmly enough and work loose.

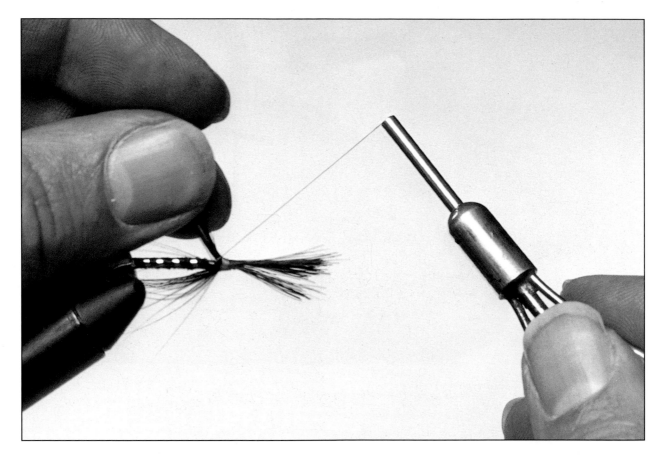

ABOVE: Lift up the wing to take a locking turn around it.

What has to be done is to remove the under-fur and this is easily accomplished by holding the section of hair by its tips and gently pulling the under-fur free from it. You will be surprised how much comes away.

In the right hand, the prepared hair wing can now be offered up to the hook and its length adjusted so that its tips come to just beyond the bend of the hook. Now you can tie it in with the pinch and loop.

It is quite a lot easier to tie in these feather fibre wings but once you have got the hair bunch on the tip of the hook with a few turns of thread it now needs to be locked into position. This is done by lifting up the hair wing in the left hand and passing the thread over the top and then back underneath the hair before then pulling backwards towards the eye of the hook. It has the effect of compressing the bunch of hair together and lifting it up clear of the hook shank.

Take a few turns of thread over the hair and, working towards the bend of the hook, go over this locking turn of thread and again press down the wing so that it is closer to the hook shank. The locking turn of thread is buried under these other turns and the whole wing is secure. Now you can hold it firmly in your left hand and cut off the waste ends with a taper so that when you do the tidying-up turns of thread and the whip finish it will all make a smooth fly.

Add a few coats of black varnish or dope and then a clear coat and you have a very smart lure.

BELOW: Press down the wing and tie over the locking turn.

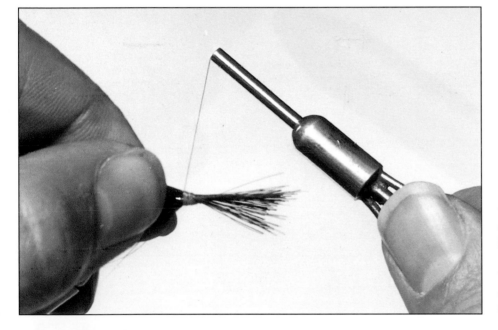

BELOW, LEFT: Cut off the waste ends of the hair wing.

BELOW, RIGHT: A whip finish on a hair wing shows its much larger bulk.

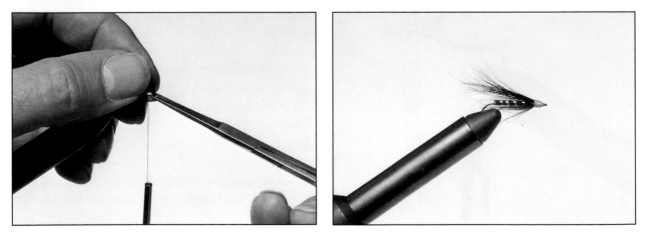

RIGHT : Pheasant tail fibres tied in for the tail.

BELOW : The abdomen wound two-thirds up the shank.

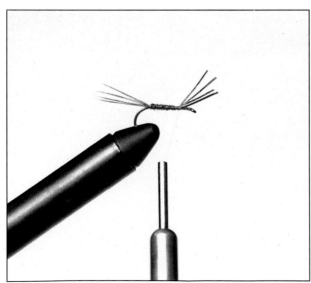

PHEASANT TAIL

Flies made from pheasant tail fibres account for huge numbers of fish every year and what would we fly tyers would do if the bird was no longer reared for sport shooting?

A nymph made from pheasant tail fibres will simulate most larval stages of aquatic insects and as a fly fisher you should certainly never be without one in your box.

We will make a classic pheasant tail nymph, so put a standard-shank hook in the vice, attach the thread and run it down to the bend of the hook. The pheasant tail feather is much like any other in that its fibres are at an angle to the main shaft, but it is very much longer and thicker.

Pull the three or four fibres with which to make the tail away from the main stem at right-angles so that the tips line up. I often use four fibres instead of three. Most nymphs have three tails but trout cannot count so if you put four on, the fly will last longer as it is usually the tails that get chewed up.

The first thing to do , then, is to tie in the tail so that the fibres are the correct length without having to spoil the whole effect of the fly by cutting them to length later on. Proportioning again! Make just the pinch and loop turns of thread to secure the fibres to the hook and then lift the remainder up away from the hook to leave the hook shank free to tie in a length of gold wire, which you must leave projecting back over the tail. Run the tying thread up the hook shank to about two-thirds of its length and then wind the pheasant tail fibres up from the tail to the thread and tie them off.

BELOW : Bending back the fibres and tying over them.

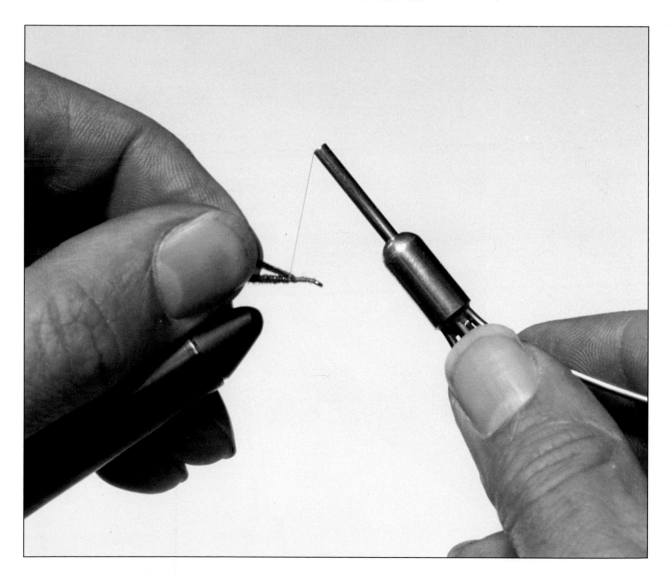

Tie them off, but do not cut them off because we have more use for them. Now you can spiral up the gold wire in the opposite direction and again remember about proportioning, doing about six turns so that segmentation is simulated.

Tie off and cut the gold wire. The next part is very important if you want to achieve a good-looking fly. It entails bending the remainder of the pheasant tail fibres back towards the tail of the fly and taking turns of thread over them so that they are tied down to the point where the body actually finishes. Fail to do this and you get a gap between abdomen and thorax which looks terrible.

Still using pheasant tail fibres you now cut off a few more and tie them in by their tips and, just as you tied in

RIGHT: Winding on the thorax.

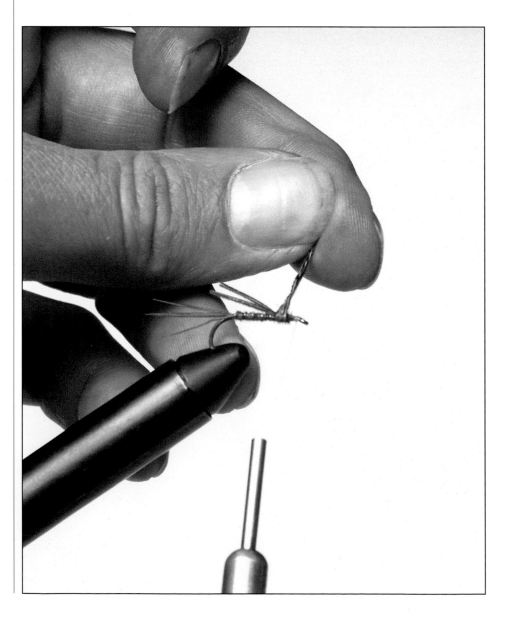

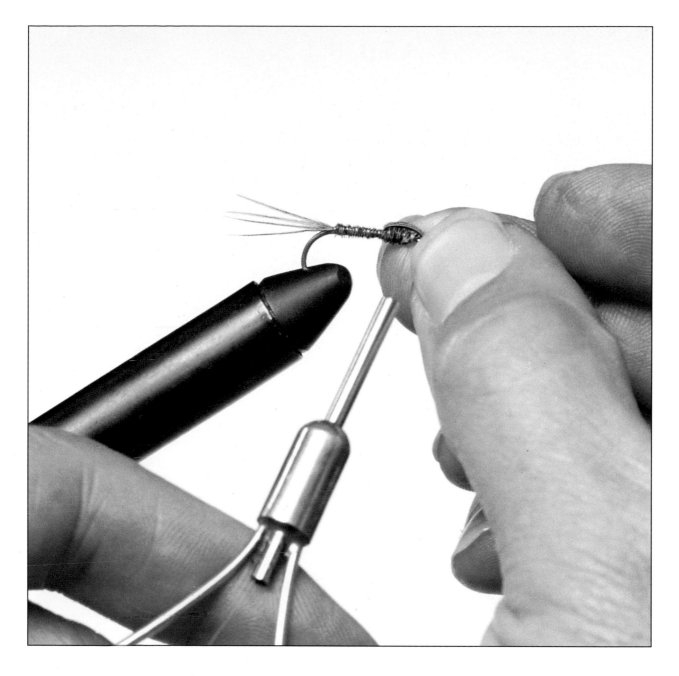

ABOVE: Fibres pulled over to make the wing cases.

the peacock herl in the very first fly, you lie them alongside the thread and wind the whole lot on so as to form a ball of a thorax. The thread which now twists in with the fibres strengthens them and prevents unravelling should a trout's teeth cut any of the fibres.

Tie off this twist of fibres just close to the hook eye and cut away the waste ends before bringing the remaining fibre ends over the top of the newly formed thorax to form the thorax case. Tie them down, cut off the excess and the fly is then ready for a whip finish and is complete, a pheasant tail nymph. There are endless variations on this pattern but this is the basis of them all.

DUBBING

I have left what is probably the most feared aspect of fly tying to the last if only because it merely follows on in a logical progression of techniques and once you have mastered this the last of my preliminary fly tying techniques you are ready to tackle virtually any fly.

Dubbing involves the application of individual fibres of hair to the tying thread which is then wound round the body or thorax of the fly to be tied and in so doing the hairs become trapped by the thread and stand out from the hook as a sort of fuzz. I taught myself how to dub and it was a long and painful process during which I tried all sorts of ways of getting those horrible bits of fur to stay attached to the thread, some more successful than others.

I tried using the liquid wax to make the thread more tacky, this was in the days before prewaxed threads, and succeeded in making everything else but the fur into a sticky mass. It was many years before I devised the technique I have used ever since and it came about when I first started commercially to tie flies for Taff Price. Speed was of the essence then and one day, when trying to be quick, I suddenly found that I could dub very easily indeed and have since demonstrated this method to club meetings and shows over many years and it has won many converts, especially among newcomers to fly tying.

I will first describe the technique and then we will use it to make a nymph.

Put a hook in the vice, a long-shank pattern, and attach the thread anywhere along the shank.

Take a pinch of the seal's fur substitute, any colour will do at this stage, and fold it up between your fingers so as to crush and bend the fibres. Squash it up until you can roll it in the palm of your hand and it will stay like a little ball, Now all the fibres are mangled and squashed and grip each other very well. Take hold of a piece of this ball and gradually tease the fibres out until you get what looks like a stretched-out web of material. It holds together very well, all the fibres gripping each other with their little bends and kinks.

RIGHT: Hair to be used for a dubbed body.

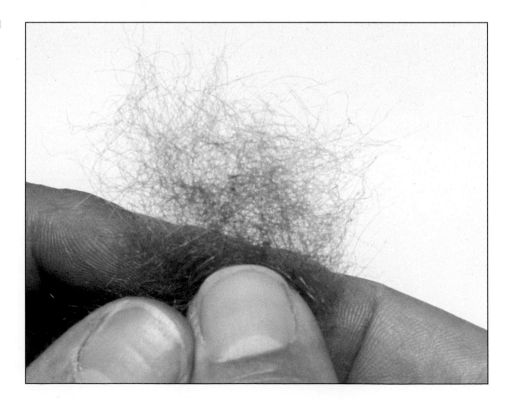

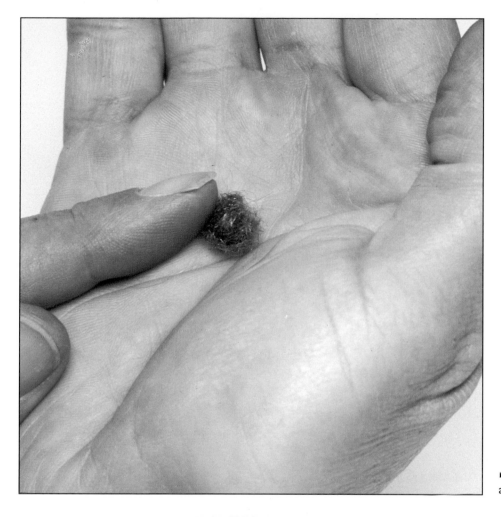

LEFT: The fibres folded and rolled into a tight ball.

RIGHT: The ball teased out to make a web of fibres.

RIGHT : The web of fibres on the thread and trapped by the left thumb.

BELOW : The web being twisted around the thread.

Lay this web of material on top of the tying thread with one end touching the hook shank and place your left thumb on the end so that it is trapped against the hook. You can now let go with the right hand and the fibre web will stay hanging from the hook.

Now twist the web of hairs round the tying thread in one direction only, clockwise, and it will very quickly form a rope with the thread.

Use the thumb and middle finger of your right hand, having first wetted each one with your tongue. Gently twist the web round the thread for two turns and then apply more pressure to twist it round the thread quite firmly. As you do so you must slowly move your fingers down the thread while all the time keeping the left thumb in position.

When the rope of material has formed you can thin it out by pulling the web of hair apart slightly and twisting again. When you are satisfied with the rope, i.e. it is nice and evenly spread with the hairs, you can now take one turn round the hook shank which will have the effect of trapping the end fibres formerly held by your left thumb and you are now free to wind the rope of hair round the hook to make the dubbed body.

It is quite easy to make the whole of a long-shank 8 body in one operation with this method and if, as you wind the rope along the shank it begins to loosen, it is a simple matter to tighten the twist. You can put on as much or as little as you like and the whole lot will cling together very well. The use of very short-fibred hair is not quite so easy with this technique and it is better to learn with hair which has a fibre length of ½- to one-in or more. From the materials in our basic selection it is possible to put together a very effective nymph using a dubbed body.

LEFT: The rope effect of the twisted web.

A B O V E : Take a turn around the hook to trap the ends previously held by the left thumb.

L E F T : The completed body, with the dubbing being picked out.

Start by tying in a tail of cock pheasant feather fibres, four or five will do, and then tie in a length of gold wire which will be the ribbing later on.

The body can now be made of dubbed green seal's fur substitute prepared exactly as I have just described, and with the rope wound so as to produce a taper to the body, i.e. thin at the tail and getting thicker up towards the eye. Take the dubbing about two-thirds of the way up the shank and finish it off before winding up the gold wire rib on the opposite spiral. On this kind of body you can see clearly how the ribbing would disappear into the body material if wound in the same direction.

Tie off the ribbing and then for the remaining third of the shank length dub on some of the brown seal's fur substitute and finally finish off with a brown hen hackle.

Once again emphasising that proportioning is all-important when making dubbed bodies and for a nymph the adage of two-thirds abdomen and one-third thorax will always hold true but you should try to achieve a neatly tapering body rather than a bulky one. If a pattern calls for the appearance of bulk then it is a simple matter to pick out the hairs with the dubbing needle, for that is its true purpose.

Although we are imitating or suggesting nymphs with our tyings it so happens time and time again that the best pattern proves to be the shaggiest-looking one which when compared with the natural creature bears no resemblance, but is this not what fly fishing is all about? It is the taking of a fish on a creation of fur and feather.

With dubbing mastered, the basics of fly tying are now complete and at this stage in a series of lessons I would usually ask my class to tie up a pattern combining most of the techniques may have learnt, just to show how well each one has progressed from the early fumblings with peacock herl and a black hen feather.

Bearing in mind the limitations of our initial material list, I think that a split-wing pheasant tail would be a good test, so here is the layout of the pattern and an example in the photograph.

Hook: Size 12 up-eye
Tail: Three fibres of cock pheasant (rooster) tail
Rib: Fine gold wire
Body: Three fibres of cock pheasant wound for two-thirds of the shank
Wings: Grey mallard tied upright and split
Hackle: Red game cock

FLY PATTERNS

Test Magnificence in the shape of a 5lb brown and a rainbow from the Mecca of fly fishers the world over, Hampshire's River Test.

This last section comprises a broad selection of flies from the four categories of patterns. The text lists suggested hook sizes and the component tying of the pattern, along with a brief description of best conditions for using each fly.

Changing from hen to cock hackles will convert the patterns to simple dry flies. An all black fly with a silver rib becomes a Williams Favourite. Change the tail to red wool and palmer up a cock hackle and you have a Zulu, a red wool body and tail with a palmered, red game, cock hackle becomes a Soldier Palmer. You will soon concoct your own variations on the basic theme and believe me – they will catch fish.

Returning a fly-caught Chinook to the Wind River in Washington.

STANDARD
WET FLIES

ABOVE: A fresh run grilse (Atlantic Salmon) from
the River Drowse in Ireland, caught on a Teeny Nymph.

~~~~~~ LIGHT CAHILL ~~~~~

A long established American wet fly, equally effective in dry or nymph form; all tyings are included here because of its all round fish-taking ability.

Hook: 16-8 standard shank
Tail: cream hackle fibres
Body: cream seals fur sub
Hackle: ginger hen hackle tied false
Wing: wood duck fibres

~~~~~~ ALEXANDRA ~~~~~~

This is a showy fly which imitates nothing and yet in true wet fly mould it is a remarkable fish catcher. Many times the colour combination of red, black and silver will occur in fly patterns.

Hook: 6-12 standard shank
Tail: red feather fibres
Body: flat silver tinsel
Hackle: black hen tied false
Wing: peacock sword feathers with slips of red feather alongside

~~ PARMACHENE BELLE ~~

An attractor wet fly that is pleasing to look at, demanding to tie and deadly when fished in bright sun and clear water. Use a long leader and fish it very slowly just under the surface.

Hook: 12-8 standard shank
Tail: red and white cock hackle fibres
Body: yellow floss with flat gold rib
Hackle: red and white cock fibres tied false
Wing: married strips of red and white goose

~~~~~~~ HORNBERG~~~~~~~

I don't think that this fly knows quite whether to be a dry, wet, or lure, but fished as a wet fly it works well and is so different that the fish maybe take it out of curiosity.

Hook: 12-8 standard shank
Body: flat silver tinsel
Wing: silver mallard feather with the tips varnished to bring them together and with cheeks of jungle cock or substitute
Hackle: ginger or cree cock hackle wound full

~~~ WICKHAM'S FANCY ~~~

A pattern that fishes well when caddis flies are on the move or as a general attractor all year round and the basis of the early stages in this book.

Hooks: 16-8 standard shank
Tail: red game cock hackle fibres
Body: gold tinsel with wire rib
Hackle: palmered red game cock
Wing: grey mallard

~~~~~~~ INVICTA ~~~~~~~

Another famous pattern for when the adult caddis/sedge are on the move, particularly in the evenings. Not an easy pattern to tie well; an excellent test of skills.

Hooks: 14-8 standard shank
Tail: golden pheasant crest
Body: dubbed yellow/amber seals fur sub with a palmered red game cock hackle and an oval gold rib
Hackle: blue jay tied false
Wing: hen pheasant centre tail

~ TEAL BLUE AND SILVER ~

Not many patterns use blue but it is very attractive to fresh migratory fish and this fly is a special for sea trout, the migratory form of browns.

Hooks: 14-8 standard shank
Tail: golden pheasant tippets
Body: silver tinsel with wire rib
Hackle: blue hen tied false
Wing: teal flank feathers

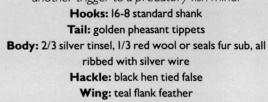

~~~~~ PETER ROSS ~~~~~

Just look at the colour combination again but this time combined with the striped effect, which is another trigger to a predatory fish mind.

Hooks: 16-8 standard shank
Tail: golden pheasant tippets
Body: 2/3 silver tinsel, 1/3 red wool or seals fur sub, all ribbed with silver wire
Hackle: black hen tied false
Wing: teal flank feather

~MALLARD AND CLARET~

Particularly good early in the season on river or lake and when chironomids are hatching.

Hooks: 16-8 standard shank
Tail: golden pheasant tippets
Body: claret seals fur sub or wool with gold rib
Hackle: claret or black hen
Wing: bronze mallard

~~~~~~~~ ZULU ~~~~~~~~

The black, red, and silver combination again. A great favourite in waters that are poor food producers and where the fish have to be opportunist feeders.

Hooks: 16-8 standard shank
Tail: red wool
Body: black wool or seals fur sub
Hackle: black cock, sometimes palmered

~~~~~~~~ BIBIO ~~~~~~~~

Just how many permutations are possible. Here is another deadly pattern using the primary trout colours.

Hooks: 12-8 standard shank
Body: black seals fur sub or wool with small red section in the middle
Hackle: black cock palmered with a silver wire rib

~~~~ SOLDIER PALMER ~~~~

A marvellous fly for the top dropper position on a wet fly cast as if fished in the surface film it resembles an insect struggling to emerge.

Hooks: 16-8 standard shank
Body: dubbed red seals fur substitute
Hackle: red game cock palmered with gold wire rib

~~~ WATSON'S FANCY ~~~

Yet another in the black/red/silver mould and a real test of a fly tier's skills. I once had to make 12 dozen of this one in size 16 for an order; what a job that was.

Hook: 14-8 standard shank
Tail: golden pheasant crest
Body: half black, half red wool with silver rib
Hackle: black hen tied false
Wing: slips of black crow with cheeks of jungle cock

~ WOODCOCK AND GREEN ~

A tried and tested pattern that is very good when fished in the upper layers during a hatch from stillwater.

Hook: 16-8 standard shank
Tail: golden pheasant tippets
Body: green seals fur sub ribbed with gold tinsel
Hackle: pale green tied false
Wing: woodcock wing quills

~~~~~~ KINGSMILL ~~~~~~ GREEN BUTT

A fluo green butt in association with a black-based fly makes a deadly combination and in this standard wet-fly form, you have in effect a mini modern lure.

Hook: 14-10 standard shank
Tail: golden pheasant crest
Body: fluo green floss butt followed by silver ribbed black ostrich herl
Hackle: black hen tied false
Wing: black crow with jungle cock cheeks and golden pheasant crest topping

~~~~ BLACK PENNELL ~~~~

One of the best flies I know when chironomids are hatching on lakes; in larger sizes it takes sea trout and tied bushy is a great dapping fly.

Hook: 14-8 standard shank
Tail: golden pheasant tippets
Body: butt of silver wire then ribbed over black floss
Hackle: black cock tied long in the fibre

~ CINNAMON AND GOLD ~

This lovely old pattern is not only a good fish catcher it's also good to look at and satisfying to tie.

Hook: 12-8 standard shank
Tail: golden pheasant tippets
Body: flat gold tinsel
Hackle: ginger cock hackle fibres tied false
Wing: cinnamon hen wing quills

~ WILLIAM'S FAVOURITE ~

If times are hard on your favourite fishery or you are on a new water then use this pattern, it's back to basics with black and silver and it works time after time.

Hook: 16-10 standard shank
Tail: black hackle fibres
Body: black floss ribbed with silver wire
Hackle: black hen

~~~~~~~ DUNKELD ~~~~~~~

Tied in larger sizes and even up to salmon size this is a great fly for a bit of flash and glitter, especially good on sunny days worked through the top layers of water.

Hooks: 16-8 standard shank
Tail: golden pheasant crest
Body: gold tinsel with wire rib
Hackle: hot orange cock tied false
Wing: bronze mallard

~~~~~~~ BUTCHER ~~~~~~~

Once again the combination of black, red and silver, this is not an easy pattern to tie well because of the difficult wing material, but it is an excellent fish catcher.

Hooks: 16-8 standard shank
Tail: red ibis substitute
Body: silver tinsel with wire rib
Hackle: black hen tied false
Wing: blue mallard

~~~~ SILVER INVICTA ~~~~

A look at the best flies on fishery reports will see this pattern come to prominence in July when the coarse fish are around and it is an excellent imitation of a pin fry as well as being a good all round pattern.

Hook: 14-8 standard shank
Tail: golden pheasant crest
Body: silver tinsel with palmered red game cock hackle and wire rib
Hackle: blue jay fibres tied false
Wings: hen pheasant centre tail feathers

~~~~~ HENDRICKSON ~~~~~

Although conceived as a nymph this fly has adapted well to tying as a wet and is now a classic North American pattern for freestone waters.

Hook: 12-8 standard shank
Tail: wood duck flank fibres
Body: dark grey/brown for dubbing with brown thread rib
Hackle: brown partridge
Wing: wood duck flank fibres

~~~ GREENWELLS GLORY ~~~

This fly has been around a long time and caught many trout for anglers all over the world and I am quite sure will continue to do so as long as there are trout to be caught.

Hook: 14-8 standard shank
Tail: greenwell hen hackle fibres (ginger with black centre and sometimes omitted)
Body: yellow tying thread darkened with wax and ribbed with golden wire
Hackle: hen greenwell tied false
Wing: starling dyed brownish green

L U R E S

Timeless elegance, a river
keeper's hut on the River
Kennet, England.

~~~~~ J E R S E Y H E R D ~~~~~

An English reservoir pattern attributed to Tom Ivens. An excellent all-round fly, but at its best around fry time at the back end of the year.

Hook: 6-20 longshank
Tail, back and head: peacock herl
Body: copper coloured tinsel
Hackle: hot orange cock wound full

~~~~~ L I G H T S P R U C E ~~~~~

A commonly used streamer pattern for trout on the West coast of America but almost unknown in the UK.

Hook: 6-10 longshank
Tail: peacock sword feather
Body: red floss and peacock herl
Hackle: badger cock wound full
Wing: badger cock hackles tied streamer style

~~~~ S I L V E R D A R T E R ~~~~

An American favourite that has found success all over the world and is especially good in broken water.

Hook: 6-10 longshank
Tail: silver mylar tubing
Hackle: peacock sword feather

~~~ M U D D L E R M I N N O W ~~~

Originally created by Don Gapen in the USA to imitate a small minnow in the streams, and now in a wide variety of options. Effective bumbled over the bottom or stripped over the surface.

Hook: 6-10 longshank
Tail: oak turkey (use hen pheasant centre tail as a sub)
Body: flat gold tinsel with wire rib
Wing: grey squirrel sheathed with oak turkey
Head: deer hair flared and clipped

~~~~~ MRS SIMPSON ~~~~~

An unusual style of fly of which there are a number of varieties all of which involved feathers tied in along the sides of the hook. Gives a very dense silhouette to the fly.

Hook: 6-10 longshank
Tail: black squirrel tail
Body: red floss
Hackle: three pairs of cock pheasant body feathers tied in at intervals along the shank

~~ BLACK AND ORANGE ~~ MARABOU

One of Taff Price's inventions that has taken a great many fish by exploiting the amazing mobility of marabou.

Hook: 6-10 longshank
Tail: orange cock hackle fibres
Body: flat gold tinsel with oval rib
Hackle: orange cock hackle fibres
Wing: black marabou sometimes with jungle cock cheeks

~~~~ WOOLLY BUGGER ~~~~

Very simple pattern and yet quite deadly, especially in cold water when fished low and deep. Must be the easiest to tie.

Hook: 10-6 longshank
Tail: black hackle fibres
Body: black chenille with palmered black hackle

~~~~ YELLOW MATUKA ~~~~

A New Zealand pattern which catches well anywhere but especially where trout feed on bait fish in lakes.

Hook: 6-10 longshank
Tail and wing: well marked hen greenwell feathers
Body: yellow floss ribbed with oval gold
Hackle: hen greenwell

~~~~ BLACK MARABOU ~~~~ MUDDLER

Yet another muddler variant and, surprise, surprise, here is the red, black and silver combination again.

Hook: 6-10 longshank
Tail: red feather fibres
Body: flat silver tinsel with wire rib
Wing: black marabou fibres
Head: deer hair flared and clipped

~~~~ ACE OF SPADES ~~~~

Essentially a black lure variant but tied matuka style with an overwing so as to give a solid profile and prevent the wing tangling under the hook bend.

Hook: 6-10 longshank
Tail and back: hen hackles dyed black
Rib: oval silver tinsel
Hackle: guinea fowl tied false
Over wing: bronze mallard

~~~~ DAVES SCULPIN ~~~~

A muddler variation which works well when fished slow and deep, particularly for older, well established fish that have turned completely predatory.

Hook: 10-4 longshank
Body: creamy yellow wool
Wing: matuka style cree cock
Rib: oval gold
Over wing: brown squirrel fibres
Fins: hen pheasant body feathers
Head: bands of coloured deer hair tied muddler style

~~~~ DOG NOBBLER ~~~~

This is a modern variation of an early type of jig fly and which is very effective on newly stocked trout. The undulating action of the tail induced by the lead head makes the fly swim enticingly.

Hook: 6-10 standard or longshank with a split shot crimped and glued to the head
Tail: bunch of marabou fibres, any colour and related to rest of fly
Body: chenille with palmered cock hackle and tinsel over rib
Head: eye effect painted on the shot

~~~~~ **B L A C K   G H O S T** ~~~~~
*Wherever fish feed on fry the black ghost will catch
them. It is a truly excellent pattern from the US.*
Hook: 6-10 longshank
Tail: yellow hackle fibres or golden pheasant crest
Body: black floss ribbed with silver oval or flat
False hackle: yellow cock hackle fibres
Wing: four white cock hackle fibres tied streamer-style

~~~~~~~ **W H I S K Y** ~~~~~~~
*Orange is a wonderful colour for rainbow trout,
especially in the summer months. It can provoke the
fish into quite literally attacking the fly. The whisky fly
is a great lure and a simple pattern to tie.*
Hook: 6-12 longshank
Tail: hot orange cock hackle fibres
Body: gold tinsel with rib of flou orange floss
Hackle: hot orange cock tied false
Wing: orange calf or squirrel tail

~~~~~ **S W E E N Y   T O D D** ~~~~~
*A Richard Walker invention using the time-
honoured colour combination of red, black and
silver to make a modern and highly effective lure.*
Hook: 6-20 longshank
Body: black floss with oval silver rib
Collar: neon magenta floss
Hackle: red cock fibres tied false
Wing: black squirrel tail

~~~~~ **M I C K Y   F I N N** ~~~~~
*This is a great pattern for the aggressive rainbow
when the water warms up and they will chase a fly;
but it also works well for many other species,
specially when the water is coloured.*
Hook: 6-10 longshank
Body: Flat silver ribbed with oval silver
Wing: in three parts, yellow, red and yellow bucktail,
squirrel for the smaller sizes

~~~~~ MUNRO KILLER ~~~~~

A hair wing version of modern salmon flies that is easy to make and every bit as effective as complicated feather wing patterns.

Hook: 4-12 up eye salmon iron

Tag: oval gold

Body: black floss with oval gold rib

Hackle: hot orange cock and dyed blue guinea fowl

Wing: yellow bucktail with black over, squirrel for smaller flies

~~~~~ BLUE CHARM ~~~~~

This is a recognised salmon fly but in reality is just a lure and shows how salmon flies can be simply tied with feather wings. Actually quite difficult to get well proportioned.

Hook: 4-12 up eye salmon

Tag: oval silver

Tail: golden pheasant crest and black ostrich as a butt

Body: black floss with oval silver rib

Hackle: blue cock

Wing: bronze mallard with teal over wing and golden pheasant crest as a topping

~~~~~ POLYSTICKLE ~~~~~

Another Richard Walker pattern which is intended to imitate a small fish and show its translucence. It comes under the general heading of lures and as you can see uses very little natural material in its tying.

Hook: 6-12 longshank

Tail and back: raffene

Body: black floss rib over silver then red floss and all over wound with strip of clear polythene

Hackle: red or orange cock hackle tied false

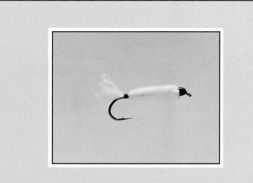

~~~~~~ APPETIZER ~~~~~~
A white based English pattern which is an excellent lure for fry feeders and makes use of the mobility of marabou for its enticing action.
Hook: 6-10 longshank
Tail: mixed fibres of silver mallard, orange and green cock hackle fibres
Body: white chenille ribbed with silver oval
Hackle: same mix as tail and tied false
Wing: white marabou with grey squirrel over

~~~~~~ BABY DOLL ~~~~~~
So called because it was apparently first tied using the white wool from baby's clothes, this pattern is tied in a fish shape, but it relies on the glow of the white wool to attract fish. White has always been a good lure colour, especially at fry time.
Hook: 6-10 long or standard shank
Tail, body, back: all of white 'baby' wool

~~~ ROYAL COACHMAN ~~~
BUCKTAIL
A North American variation on an old pattern which has turned an already good fly into an excellent lure.
Hook: 6-10 longshank
Tail: golden pheasant tippetts
Body: red floss with ends of peacock herl
Hackle: brown cock tied false
Wing: white bucktail fibres

~~~~~ PEARL ZONKER ~~~~~

The technique of using strips of fur tied in Matuka style is very popular nowadays; the pearl mylar tubing makes a great fish scale effect.

Hook: 4-10 longshank
Body: pearl mylar tubing
Wing: thin strip of white rabbit tied matuka style at either end of the body
Hackle: red cock wound full

~~~ CAT'S WHISKER ~~~~

Another white-based fly for fry feeders and mated with fluo yellow chenille to deadly effect.

Hook: 6-10 longshank
Tail: tuft of white marabou
Body: fluo yellow chenille
Wing: tuft of white marabou
Head: pair of bead chain eyes

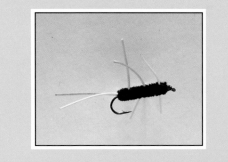

~~~~~ GIRDLE BUG ~~~~~~

Born from a type of Bass fly, this is an American pattern through and through. Quite what it represents I doubt that anyone knows but fish take it well. I once had an Irish salmon on one.

Hook: 4-12 longshank
Tail and legs: white or black living rubber
Body: chenille in a range of colours

NYMPHS

Fresh from the sea, a 25-inch
Char caught in Alaska.

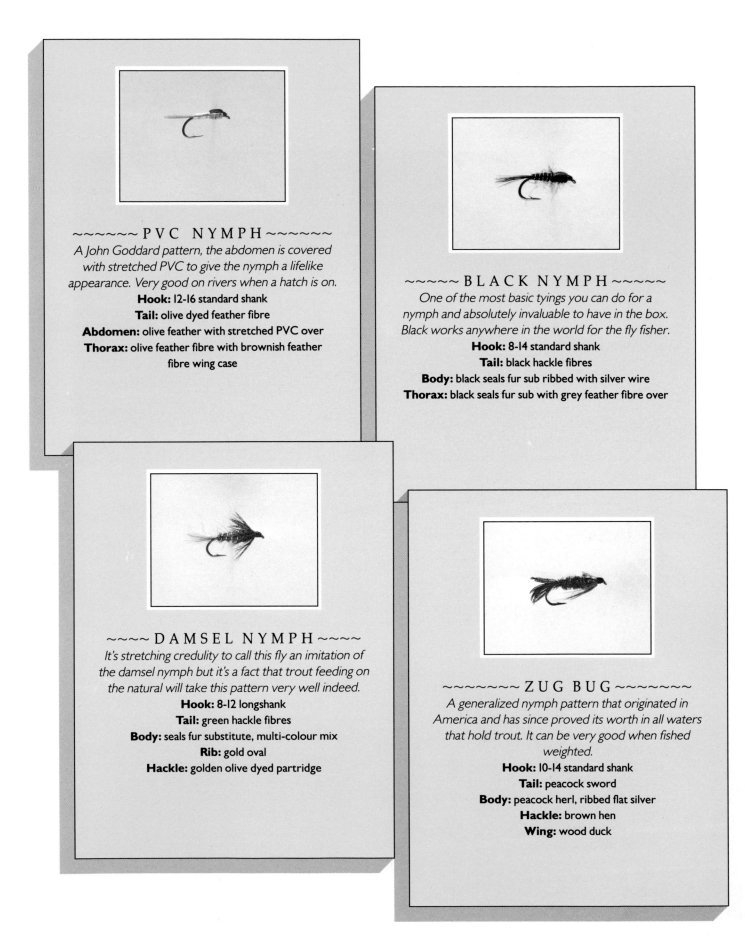

~~~~~~ PVC NYMPH ~~~~~~

A John Goddard pattern, the abdomen is covered with stretched PVC to give the nymph a lifelike appearance. Very good on rivers when a hatch is on.

Hook: 12-16 standard shank
Tail: olive dyed feather fibre
Abdomen: olive feather with stretched PVC over
Thorax: olive feather fibre with brownish feather fibre wing case

~~~~~ BLACK NYMPH ~~~~~

One of the most basic tyings you can do for a nymph and absolutely invaluable to have in the box. Black works anywhere in the world for the fly fisher.

Hook: 8-14 standard shank
Tail: black hackle fibres
Body: black seals fur sub ribbed with silver wire
Thorax: black seals fur sub with grey feather fibre over

~~~~ DAMSEL NYMPH ~~~~

It's stretching credulity to call this fly an imitation of the damsel nymph but it's a fact that trout feeding on the natural will take this pattern very well indeed.

Hook: 8-12 longshank
Tail: green hackle fibres
Body: seals fur substitute, multi-colour mix
Rib: gold oval
Hackle: golden olive dyed partridge

~~~~~~~ ZUG BUG ~~~~~~~~

A generalized nymph pattern that originated in America and has since proved its worth in all waters that hold trout. It can be very good when fished weighted.

Hook: 10-14 standard shank
Tail: peacock sword
Body: peacock herl, ribbed flat silver
Hackle: brown hen
Wing: wood duck

~~~~ SWANNUNDAZE ~~~~
STONEFLY

An excellent pattern that makes full use of the translucence obtained by the use of swannundaze, a plastic which is flat one side and oval on the other.

Hook: 6-8 longshank, bent to suggest the humped pupa
Tail: brown goose biots
Abdomen: mixed golden yellow and grey seals fur sub dubbed heavily and ribbed with amber swannundaze
Thorax: similar dubbing mix with the wing cases being formed by laying a brown speckled partridge feather along the back and overlaying a striped partridge feather

~~~~~~~~ PRINCE ~~~~~~~~

An interesting fly in that it looks 'buggy' and yet actually resembles nothing specific. The white feather slips seem to act as an attractant to the fish.

Hook: 8-12 standard shank
Tail: brown goose biot
Body: peacock herl with flat gold rib
Hackle: brown hen
Horns: slips of white goose or swan

~~~ MONTANA NYMPH ~~~

A dressing of the Stone Fly Larva initiated in Montana and now used worldwide. A general-purpose pattern where the Stone Fly does not occur and in Europe it is little other than a variant of the black lure.

Hook: 12-8 longshank, often weighted
Tail: black cock hackle tips or bunch of black cock hackle fibres
Abdomen: black chenille
Thorax: yellow chenille with variants using fluo green, white or orange
Wing case: black chenille
Hackle: Black cock wound through the thorax

~~~~~ GOLD RIBBED ~~~~~
HARE'S EAR

This is a fly that catches any trout that is feeding on ephemerid (mayfly) nymphs, and also works as a general nymph pattern right throughout the year.

Hook: 8-16 standard shank
Tail: ginger hackle fibres or longer hairs from a hare's mask
Body: dubbed hare's ear ribbed with gold tinsel
Thorax: dubbed hare's ear picked out with feather fibre wing case

~~ AMERICAN MARABOU ~~ DAMSEL

This tying has become amazingly successful in the UK in recent years. It really comes into its own when the damsel larvae are active during the main part of the day.

Hook: 8-12 longshank
Tail: tuft of olive marabou fibres
Abdomen: twisted olive marabou
Thorax: dubbed olive seals fur sub with short-fibred olive hackle half way through and wing cases of olive feather fibre
Head: bright green beads

~~~~~ SAWYER'S PTN ~~~~~

A classic the world over and a remarkably effective nymph dressing. Invented by Frank Sawyer, the river keeper from Hampshire, England. Unusual in that the tying thread is replaced by fine copper wire which acts as the pattern's weight.

Hook: 10-18 standard shank
Tail, body and thorax: pheasant tail (rooster) fibres

~ MEDIUM ALL PURPOSE ~ NYMPH

This pattern is the American equivalent of the English angler's GRHE, it typifies the greater variety of detail of American flies in that it comes in three shades.

Hook: 8-12 longshank
Tail: pheasant tail fibres
Body: grey brown polydubbing ribbed with clear nylon
Wing case: grouse hackle with the ends bent back to form the legs

~~~~~ EARLY BROWN ~~~~~ STONEFLY

An ideal pattern for the streams where the stonefly features strongly in the fish diet.

Hook: 8-10 longshank
Tail: brown hen hackle fibres
Abdomen: dubbed grey rabbit underfur with a pale plastic rib
Thorax: grey rabbit underfur mixed with guard hairs well picked out and with wing cases of pale brown feather fibre

~~~~~ CASED CADDIS ~~~~~

Larvae of the stonefly (caddis) make up the greater part of a trout's diet, especially in the early season, and imitations of the larval form fished along the bottom are very successful.

Hook: 8-12 longshank
Body: blue underfur from a rabbit dubbed onto silver tinsel chenille and wound
Head: black ostrich herl

~~~~~ TEENY NYMPH ~~~~~

Invented by Oregon's steelhead king, Jim Teeny, this fly was to be a broad band pattern suitable for all species and simple to tie so there would be no fear of fishing it in snaggy places. Tied in a variety of colours and only using rooster (cock pheasant) tail fibres.

Hook: 12 short shank to 2 longshank
Body, false hackles: tail feather fibres from a rooster (cock pheasant) sometimes tied with a wing of the same material on the larger hooks

~~~~~ GREEN BITCH ~~~~~
CREEK NYMPH

A modern American tying using living rubber for its action; a general stone fly pattern.

Hook: 6-10 longshank
Tail: two pieces of living rubber
Body: woven from fluo green and black chenille
Thorax: black chenille with red game cock hackle palmered through it
Head: two more pieces of living rubber

~ COCKWILLS RED BROWN ~

Based on a reservoir pattern by the late Tom Ivens and intended to represent the coloration of the male stickleback at breeding time, this fly has proved to be a very good general-purpose nymph for most stillwaters.

Hook: 10 longshank
Tail, back and head: four fibres of peacock herl
Body: copper golfingering ribbed with a strand of brown ostrich herl and copper wire
Thorax: two turns of neon magenta chenille

~~ GREEN THORAX PTN ~~

A variant on the pheasant tail series and using green fluo which attracts trout so well. Used as a general purpose nymph or fished fast at fry time.

Hook: 8-12 longshank
Tail: pheasant tail fibres
Body: pheasant tail fibres ribbed with copper wire
Thorax: fluo green floss with pheasant fibres over
Hackle: ginger cock tied false

~~ COLONEL'S CREEPER ~~

An all-purpose nymph that would make an excellent stonefly imitation and has found great success in English stillwaters.

Hook: 8-10 longshank
Tail: bunch of olive dyed rabbit fur
Body: weighted along the sides of the hook to widen it then dubbed olive seals fur sub ribbed with nylon
Thorax: dressed upside down and made with two wing cases of varnished raffene and legs of olive goose biots in among the dubbed olive seals fur sub

~~~~~~~ LEAD BUG ~~~~~~~

One of the author's patterns and designed for use on large fish which can be targetted in clear water. It gives a very approximate suggestion of a nymph, with its segmented body and thorax hump, and is intended to sink very rapidly, yet not be too heavy.

Hook: 10 to 12 standard shank
Tail: olive floss
Abdomen: fine lead wire
Thorax, wing case and leg stubs: olive floss

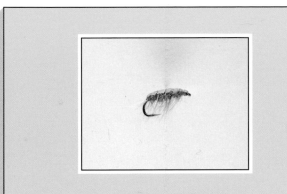

~~~~ GOLDEN SHRIMP ~~~~

The shrimp is a drab greenish or brown hue, although when changing its skin it is very much paler; many anglers feel that the golden shrimp somehow appears to be vulnerable to the trout. Whatever the truth, the fly is very successful.

Hook: 10 or 12 standard shank, a Sedge pattern is very good
Tail: fibres of golden olive cock hackle
Body: golden olive seals fur or substitute
Hackle: palmered golden olive cock
Back: yellow dyed latex
Rib: gold wire

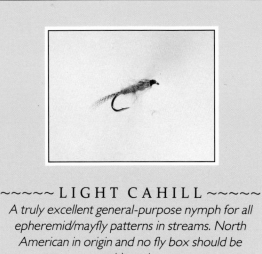

~~~~~ LIGHT CAHILL ~~~~~

A truly excellent general-purpose nymph for all epheremid/mayfly patterns in streams. North American in origin and no fly box should be without it.

Hook: 10-18 standard shank
Tail: wood duck fibres
Body: creamy seals fur substitute
Hackle: ginger hen fibres
Wing case: wood duck

~~~~ GREEN CHOMPER ~~~~

A remarkably easy pattern to tie and it can suggest all manner of aquatic life. The fish certainly think it looks edible and the colour can be varied according to water and season.

Hook: 10-14 standard shank
Back: raffene
Body: ostrich herl

DRY FLIES

Tranquility in the setting of a
small lake at Wintershall in
Surrey.

~~~~~ ROYAL WULFF ~~~~~

One of Lee Wulff's all time greats and a wonderful general purpose dry that rides rough water very well and is taken by all species.

Hook: 8-12 standard shank
Tail: black squirrel hair
Body: red floss with peacock herl either end
Wings: white calf tail
Hackle: two red game cock hackles

~~~ CINNAMON SEDGE ~~~

A very effective broad band sedge pattern, not just for when the actual cinnamon sedge is hatching. Equally effective on rivers or lakes.

Hook: 10-14 up eye
Body: cinnamon feather fibre with palmered ginger cock hackle and gold wire rib
Wings: cinnamon hen quills
Hackle: ginger cock hackle

~~ FRENCH PARTRIDGE ~~ MAYFLY

An all-time English favourite for the annual mayfly carnival when the trout gorge themselves on this large insect. There may be more efficient patterns, but this one is so pretty.

Hook: special mayfly 8-10 longshank
Tail: cock pheasant fibres
Body: natural raffia ribbed with red thread and an olive cock hackle and gold wire
Hackle: French partridge flank feather

~~~ DADDY LONG LEGS ~~~ (CRANE FLY)

A large terrestrial that trout love to eat and which in late summer can hatch in enormous numbers.

Hook: 8-12 longshank
Body: detached end of closely bunched dyed deer hair
Legs: knotted cock pheasant tail fibres
Wings: cree hackle points
Hackle: two ginger cock hackles wound full

~~~ ELK HAIR HOPPER ~~~

Hoppers are a great fly to fish in the summer in the USA when they are cast at the edges of the stream. Now they are being used in Europe but more as general purpose dries on lakes.

Hook: 8-12 longshank
Tail: red dyed squirrel hair
Body: yellow floss ribbed with clipped Grizzle hackle
Wing: bunch of elk hair
Hackle: two cree cock hackles

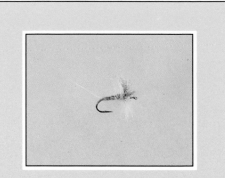

~~~~~ LIGHT CAHILL ~~~~~

Thought to be at least a hundred years old, this pattern is very effective when the paler ephemerids are hatching, especially in the evening when it is easy to see.

Hook: 12-16 standard shank
Tail: cream hackle fibres
Body: cream seals fur substitute
Wings: wood duck
Hackle: cream cock hackle

~~~~ YELLOW HUMPY ~~~~

A wonderful floater for rough water, originally from the freestone rivers of Western America.

Hook: 10-14 standard shank
Tail: moose fibres
Body: yellow floss with the moose fibres tied over the top
Wing: ends of a bunch of moose fibres
Hackle: two grizzle cock hackles

~ STRADDLEBUG MAYFLY ~

Interesting variation for mayfly in that this pattern has an orange hackle which makes it stand out from all the others. It often gets taken when the fish are full to the gills with the natural.

Hook: 8-12 longshank
Tail: cock pheasant fibres
Body: natural raffia ribbed with gold wire
Hackle: two wound together, hot orange cock and summer duck feather
Head: peacock herl

~~~~ BLACK BIVISIBLE ~~~~

A fly that relies on merely suggesting an adult insect by its straggly hackle and fuzzy outline. It has the advantage of riding very well and being easy for the angler to see and tie.

Hook: 10-14 standard shank
Tail: black cock hackle fibres
Body: palmered black cock hackle
Hackle: white cock hackle

~ RICHARD WALKER SEDGE ~

The ever inventive Richard Walker produced this pattern to have a sedge (caddis) profile; the long hackle was so that the fly could be stripped back over the surface to imitate the adults skittering motion.

Hook: 8-12 standard shank
Butt: hot orange floss
Body: cock pheasant fibres
Wing: red game cock hackle fibres
Hackle: red game cock hackle, long fibred

~~~~~~ BLACK GNAT ~~~~~~

A black dry fly is essential at times, especially in early season when the natural hatches.

Hook: 10-18 up eye
Tail: black cock hackle fibres
Body: black floss
Wings: grey mallard or starling
Hackle: black cock wound full

~~ DARK HENDRICKSON ~~

A famous standard American dry that catches well when the mayfly species hatch and scores on most waters as a general pattern.

Hook: 12-18 standard shank
Tail: dark dun or grey cock hackle fibres
Body: dubbed muskrat under fur
Wing: wood duck
Hackle: dark dun or grey cock hackle

~~~~ QUILL GORDON ~~~~
*A pattern from the Catskills in New York State,
often used in the UK as an alternative to standard
olive patterns when the natural is hatching.*
Hook: 12-18 standard shank
Tail: light brown or grey cock hackle fibres
Body: stripped peacock quill
Wings: wood duck
Hackle: medium dun cock or grey cock

~~ BLUE WINGED OLIVE ~~
*This imitation of a commonly occurring fly is a
standard for when the fly hatches and is essential for
anyone who fishes limestone (chalk) waters.*
Hook: 14-16 standard shank
Tail: dark dun hackle fibres, grey will suffice
Body: dubbed olive grey fur
Wings: blue dun hackle tips
Hackle: dark dun cock or grey hackle

~~~~~~~ ADAMS ~~~~~~~~
*This American fly is now much used on English chalk
streams, especially when olives are hatching. It also
makes a good lake dry fly.*
Hook: 10-20 standard shank
Tail: mixed brown and grizzle cock hackle fibres
Body: muskrat under fur dubbed
Wing: grizzle hackle tips
Hackle: mixed red game and grizzle

~~~ WICKHAMS FANCY ~~~
*A flashy dry fly that serves well when there is a
sedge hatch or when the water is rough and the sun
bright when its wink of gold brings the fish up.*
Hook: 16-8 standard shank
Tail: red game cock hackle fibres
Body: gold tinsel with palmered red game cock hackle
and gold wire rib
Wings: grey mallard or starling
Hackle: red game cock hackle

~BLUE PHEASANT TAIL~
A fly of the rough water rivers which are fished best early in the year and will produce fish even when there is no hatch taking place.
Hook: 14-10 standard shank
Tail: pheasant tail fibres
Body: pheasant tail fibres with gold wire rib
Hackle: blue dun cock

~~~~~GREY DUSTER~~~~~
This is a wonderful pattern when all sorts of tiny smuts are on the water and trout are being 'difficult'. It will often fool the most crafty fish and yet is simplicity itself.
Hook: 18-12 standard shank
Body: dubbed rabbit under fur 'blueish grey'
Hackle: badger cock hackle 'white with black centre and tips'

~~LUNNS PARTICULAR~~
A classic Test fly and best when olive spinners are on the water but it serves for any fall of spent fly.
Hook: 16-14 up eye
Tail: fibres of red game cock hackle
Body: stripped red game cock hackle stem
Wings: blue dun hackle points tied spent
Hackle: red game cock hackle

OLIVE ELK ~~~~~WING CADDIS~~~~~
Quite an easy pattern to tie and the elk hair splay serves well to suggest the sedge (caddis) profile as well as making the fly float well.
Hook: 14-10 standard shank
Body: dubbed yellowish for substitute
Hackle: palmered red game cock hackle
Wing: elk hair with the butts lifted to make a head

ADDITIONAL MATERIALS IN COMMON USAGE

Hackles from either cock or hen come in a wide variety of natural colours as well as the myriad of dyed ones available and a good fly tying collection should include:

Grizzle, white, badger, honey and cree cock necks

White, ginger and greenwell hen

Dyed cock and hen in shades of olive, red, claret, orange, blue, green and yellow

Natural and dyed black, yellow and bleached white deer hair

Marabou plumes (in fact from the domestic turkey) in a wide range of dyed colours

Ostrich hcrl in a range of colours

Partridge feathers, English and French

A hare's mask, i.e. the complete face of the hare for a range of excellent dubbing material

BELOW: A wide selection of feathers which will enable many patterns to be tied.

Other tinsels such as oval silver and gold and copper wire

Golden pheasant crest and neck feathers

Dyed hairs in various colours, squirrel, bucktail and goat

Condor substitute, large quill feathers dyed in various colours

Man-made materials such as chenille, raffene, latex, swannudaze, flashabou, polythene and a wide range of other items used by fly tyers

Wing quills from starling, grouse, woodcock and speckled hen

Flank feathers from teal and wood duck

Bronze mallard feathers and, from the same bird, the blue wing coverts

A whole range of dubbing materials, some natural some man-made and in a wide variety of colours

This list may seem an intimidating one but once you are dedicated to fly tying you will inevitably accumulate most of the items on this list and a good many more!

Fly tying is all about inventiveness and you will try all manner of materials in an attempt to find that deadly, sure-fire, never-failing pattern.

LEFT : A dubbing twister.

ADDITIONAL TOOLS

At the beginning of this book I suggested that you acquire two pairs of scissors, one for feather and one for tinsel and so on. Now that you are well into fly tying I suggest that you buy a really first-class pair and just keep them for your better work with small flies.

A dubbing twister is a very useful gadget for tying dubbed bodies with short-fibres furs such as mole or hare's ear. It will more than earn its keep.

A hair stacker is a tube into which you slip long hairs which are to form wings and so on, and then by tapping the tube you can ensure that all the ends of the hairs are lined up.

A gallows tool enables parachute hackles to be tied with relative ease and it is a worth-while addition to your equipment.

Being an inventive lot, fly tyers are forever bringing out 'new' gadgets but you will rarely find professional tyers using any others than those tools I have listed. If a pro does not use a tool, be sure that it is not worth buying.

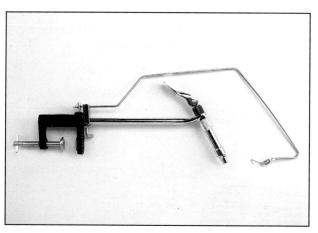

ABOVE : The Gallows tool for parachute hackles.

SPECIAL TECHNIQUES

Some of the additional materials I listed require that you learn a new method of tying in addition to the basic ones we mastered, and I will describe them now that you are able to move on to more adventurous fly tying.

DEER HAIR

This is a fun-material to use although in latter years it has been a nuisance to me as I have become allergic to it and have to take anti-histamine tablets before handling it. Deer hair is used mostly in forming the heads of Muddler patterns but has all kinds of other uses.

A single deer hair is a hollow tube and if, for example, you had a length of half an in copper pipe on a table and sharply compressed it at one point it would fold in half

LEFT: A bunch of deer hair ready for the muddler head.

and this also happens to deer hair when given the same treatment. We take a bunch of these hollow-tube hairs and compress them all at the same point so that the result is a flare of deer hair. Looked at in that context tying deer hair is no great problem. It is easiest first to tie deer hair on to a hook which only has a covering of tying thread to get the hang of the method.

Cut off a bunch of hair about as thick as a pencil, with the pointed ends projecting to your left. Offer the bunch up to the hook and lay it parallel with the shank before taking a loose turn of thread round it. Do not compress the fibre at this stage.

Make a second loose turn of thread in exactly the same place as the first and then pull slowly downwards with the bobbin and at the same time relax your hold on the bunch of hair. As the two loose turns of thread begin to tighten the bunch of hair will be compressed and start to flare out and at the same time turn round the hook shank so that by the time you have fully tightened the thread the hair will have flared all round the hook.

ABOVE: Two loose turns of thread around the bunch of hair.

RIGHT: Tightening the thread causes the hair to flare.

If making up a full head, you would form the thumb and two-finger pinch with the left hand and sweep the fibres back towards the hook bend and place a further bunch of hair on top of the hook shank. Repeat the operation to flare the hair and gradually build up a full head. It will now look like some kind of hairy monster and must be clipped to shape with scissors. You can make up your own shapes but in the photograph you will see that I have cut it to a conventional Muddler head and you can also see the reason for tying in the pointed ends of the hair off to the left. If you leave them uncut they form a rather neat collar hackle effect.

Now tie up a single Muddler using black wool for the body ribbed with silver tinsel and a wing of black squirrel hair. Make sure that when you tie off the hair that you cut its ends to a taper so that when the thread is wound over it you will get a smooth, tapering base on to which the deer hair can be spun. Some tyers use the cut-off end of a ball-pen to tap the fibres firmly down the hook shank before applying a further bunch of hair and this results in a very dense and tightly packed head which will increase the fly's buoyancy. The hollow hairs make deer hair a wonderful floatant.

BELOW : Clearing the way for additional applications of deer hair.

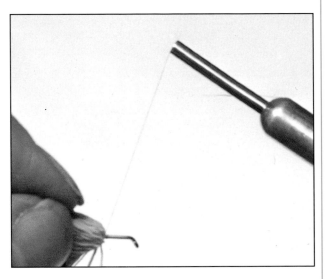

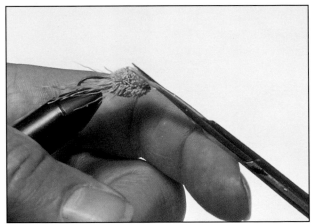

ABOVE : Muddler head clipped to shape.

LEFT : The finished muddler head.

ABOVE: A pair of hackles ready to make a streamer wing.

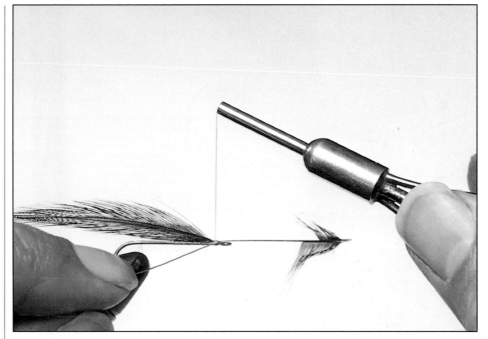

RIGHT: A streamer wing securely tied in.

S TREAMERS

This technique involves using whole hackles tied in at the head of the fly to act as a wing and a long-shank hook is normally used. It is very important to check that the hackles to be used are identical in size and colour. Two are prepared by stripping the fluff from their base and then positioned so that their natural curves make their points come together rather like a pair of hands. The pair of feathers are then gripped in the left hand and tied on top of the hook as though they were a wing, using the pinch and loop technique. Additional security can be had by turning the stems back over themselves and tying down, this locks the hackles on.

RIGHT: Prepared hackles to make a matuka wing.

ABOVE: A matuka wing tied in.

MATUKAS

Very similar to the previous technique except that the body ribbing is left unwound while the hackles are put on as for the streamer. Very often the underside of each hackle is stripped off so that when laid down on to the shank the feathers look like a crest on top of the hook. Hold the tips of the hackles in the left hand and stroke the fibres back towards the eye so that they stand up away from the quill.

Now hold the hackle down on top of the hook and commence winding the ribbing material up over the hackles so that they are bound down on to the shank. Take great care to wind between the hackle fibres so that they do not become trapped and twisted out of shape. Finally, tie off the ribbing and stroke the fibres back down. Flies tied in this way tend not to tangle as do streamers when the wing bends down under the hook and gets trapped in the bend.

MARABOU

This is a very soft and fluffy feather which when wet is amazingly mobile in water. Used as tails up to 4-in long it pulsates and wiggles as the fly is retrieved and it makes excellent wings or bodies with lots of life. An easy way to prepare it for tying in for wing or tail is to cut a

L E F T : Ribbing to secure a matuka wing.

A B O V E : A shuttlecock of marabou fibres.

section of fibres free from the main quill and to then wet the thumb and forefinger of your right hand and twist the ends of the fibres together so that they form what looks like a shuttlecock of fibres. These little 'shuttle-cocks' can then be tied in. Make a simple marabou fly by tying in a tail of black fibres then winding on a black chenille body and finally a black hen hackle. It might not look much but this pattern will catch fish the world over.

A B O V E : A marabou tail tied in.

RIGHT: Winding on to achieve a dubbed body.

BELOW: Short fibred fur in a dubbing twister loop.

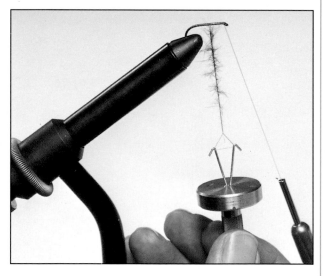

ABOVE: The twister spun to trap the fibres.

SHORT-FIBRED FURS

It is difficult to dub such material in the way I have previously described but a nice easy way is to use a dubbing twister. The idea is to have a loop of thread coming free of the body of the pattern and to hang the two loops of the twister from the thread loop. The fibres of fur are then carefully spread along the loop before the twister is spun. This twists up the thread loop and effectively traps the hairs. The twist can then be wound is just the same way as you wound the dubbing rope.

This technique does have the advantage over normal dubbing methods in that the hair fibres produce a more bulky effect and it is possible to adapt this to making a hair hackle by using guard hairs from some animals.

PARTRIDGE

These short feathers often cause a lot of trouble for fly tyers because they have a very thick base, so that if they are tied in by the base and wound round the hook they cause a lot of bulk. The correct thing to do is to stroke the fibres down from the tip to the base so that they stand out from the stem and to then tie in by the tip and wind the couple of turns necessary to get the hackle effect without having to get on to the thick part of the stem. The snag is that the feather is actually very weak and breaks easily, so it is a matter of carefully judging the amount of pressure to apply when winding the hackle.

WINGING WITH BODY FEATHERS

Wings of bronze mallard, wood duck or teal are an absolute nuisance to tie in as matched pairs because the fibres have very weak hook-and-eye systems to join them up and the whole lot will often fall apart as the pinch and loop is done. It is far better for all practical fishing purposes to stroke a section of fibres out at an angle to the stem so that the tips are all lined up and to them cut it away. The section of fibres is then folded in half and in half again before being placed between a wetted forefinger and thumb and rolled to and fro. This mixes up all the fibres to make what is called a rolled wing. This is then tied in as a whole section but still using the pinch and loop method.

BELOW: Bronze mallard feathers prepared for a bunched wing.

LEFT: Tying in a prepared partridge hackle.

Cutting off dry fly hackles

~~~~~

It is very easy when cutting off the waste tip of a fully wound hackle for a dry fly to inadvertently cut away some of the fibres which you want. One way of overcoming this is to use your best scissors and open the points by just ¼ in. Keep the points open by this amount and then slide the hackle stem into the vee made by the blades. If you now either pull down on the hackle or push up with the scissors the stem of the hackle slides into the vee and is sliced through but only the tips are cut, not any of the fibres.

There are many more refinements and specialised techniques to fly tying and as I said in the opening pages the subject can be treated as an art form with tyers entering competitions to make the most technically perfect fly or the best imitative pattern. Fly tying can open up a whole new meaning to your understanding and enjoyment of the sport of fishing and if this book has set you on that road to taking your first fish on a fly of your own tying then I wish you a steady hand, nimble fingers and a never-ending queue of fish eager to take your offerings.

Fly tyers like to retain some record of their better achievements and a way of creating an attractive addition to the home is to set a collection of patterns into a frame and hang them on your wall. I made this set of salmon and trout flies for a very good friend and some are immensely complex but yet satisfying to tie. For example, the Jock Scott is true to its original tying and has 29 different sections of feather in its wing alone.

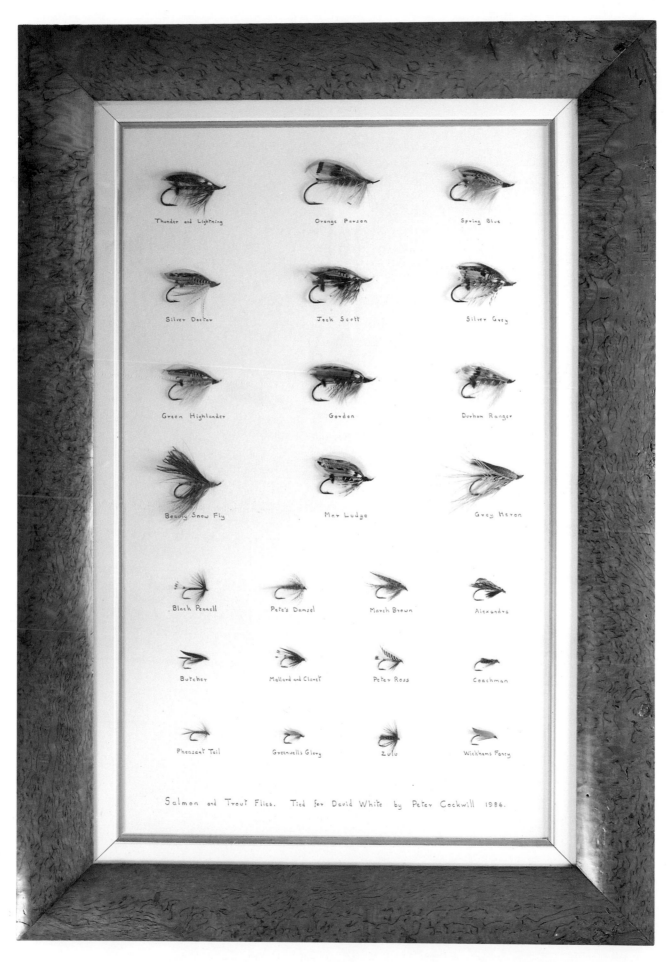

G L O S S A R Y

Abdomen: Segmented section of insect body. It does not bear legs but may have breathing filaments.

Badger: Term for colour of hackle feather, white-to-honey with black centre and tips.

Bobbin: Tool for retaining spool of thread under tension.

Caddis: Term for species of insect that makes a case to live in during the larval form. The adult is also often called a caddis fly.

Cape: The whole skin of a bird's neck up to the top of its head and complete with all the feathers.

Dubbing: Term used for the technique of applying hair to thread and then on to the body of the fly.

Dubbing needle: A needle set into a handle and used principally to pick out fibres from a dubbed body.

Ephemerid: A collective generic term for one of the largest groups of insects represented by the fly tyer.

Fibre: A single filament of feather.

Gape: The distance between the shank of a hook and the point.

Greenwell: Term for hackle colour, ginger with black centre.

Grizzle: Hackle colour, black and white barring.

Guard hair: The long hairs of a section of fur which actually are the show surface.

Hackle: Single feather from the cape or the feather when wound round the hook.

Hackle pliers: Spring-loaded tool used to grip a hackle when winding it round the hook.

Matuka: A style of dressing where the wing is bound down to the top of the hook-shank with turns of ribbing material.

Metz: Trade name for genetically reared feathers for fly tyers.

Neck: Another term for cape (which see).

Quill: The central stem of a feather or a whole feather, i.e. flight quill.

Shank: The length of a hook from the start of the bend up to the eye.

Streamer: Term for a style of dressing where the wings are long and made of hackle tied in at the head of the fly.

Thorax: The fatter part of an insect's body which carries the legs and from where the wings develop.

Tinsel: Metallic or lurex material used for ribbing or bodies.

Vice: The tool used to clamp the hook steady.

Jim Teeny with a magnificent
Chinook from Oregon.

INDEX